# the
# ins and out of
# REJECTION

By Charles R. Solomon, Ed.D.

## Heritage House Publications

7239 Mount Holy Cross
Littleton, Colorado 80127
Phone 303-979-4530

Author's note:

The scripture references quoted are from the King James Version unless otherwise noted.

––––––––––

The material in this book is designed to be used in sharing with others in conjunction with the Bible that they may see how their deepest needs may be met in the Lord Jesus Christ. It is not to be used in any professional office or practice advertised as Spirituotherapy except as duly authorized by Grace Fellowship International in Denver, Colorado.

––––––––––

Library of Congress Card Number 76-11483

First Printing,  July - 1976

Printed in the United States of America

By
Heritage House Publications
Littleton, Colorado

# DEDICATION

*To my children, Ronald, Catherine, and Susan, who suffered in varying degrees at my hand while I struggled with an invisible foe until delivered by "him who is invisible . . . ."*

*(Hebrews 11:27)*

## THE INS AND OUT OF REJECTION

Part One:  The Ways In or The Rejection Syndrome
Part Two:  The Way Out or The Cross

# contents

*Cover Art Work By* Ron Solomon
*Photograph By* Steven Hubachek

# Part 1.

# THE WAYS IN
## OR
# THE REJECTION SYNDROME

## PREFACE TO PART ONE

The author has found that persons who have mental/
emotional disturbances usually have not had their need for
love and affection met in their childhood, and the effect has
continued into their adult lives. The behavior of such persons
falls into many predictable patterns which are presented in
Part One under the heading, *The Rejection Syndrome.* Since
the need for love and acceptance is universal, the principles
laid out are applicable to all whose needs have not been met.

Illogical and bizarre behaviors have their roots in an inner
need which can usually be traced to the fact that the love
needs have not been fulfilled. Even those who have loving
and accepting parents may not feel assured of being loved in
a manner which gives them security thus making it possible
for them to succeed in life.

The symptoms which persons bring to counseling are such
things as marital conflict, emotional disturbances, mental
aberrations, teenage problems, vocational dissatisfaction, and
a host of others. Almost invariably the symptom is mistaken
for the problem, and the person may have spent twenty or
thirty years with little more than symptomatic relief. The
help he seeks is usually in the form of marriage counseling,
vocational counseling, or therapy in the offices of
psychologists or psychiatrists.

This book, along with *Handbook to Happiness* by the
author, is written to help those suffering from depression,
loneliness, discouragement, defeat or from more serious
emotional and mental symptoms understand the cause and to
provide a satisfying and lasting answer. To avoid repetition,
the material in *Handbook to Happiness* has not been included
in this book. The *Handbook* is an introduction to
Spirituotherapy®, a Christ-centered approach to counseling
which may be understood and shared with others without
the necessity of advanced formal education. Understanding

the material in it is prerequisite to deriving full benefit from this book.

Rejection is a symptom stemming from the self-centered life which is the root problem. Conventional approaches to counseling and therapy have as their goal the strengthening of the individual, helping him learn to cope with himself and his situation in life. Such goals as self-confidence, self-realization, and self-actualization are sought by the individual as he is spurred on by a "helping person." Although there may be a decrease in symptoms through counseling and therapy, the strengthening of the self-life in the individual is counterproductive in the person's spiritual life.

Although the rejection which damaged the person's life may have been experienced on a human level, the acceptance which is truly and lastingly healing must be experienced on a spiritual or divine level. We have warrant for this in the verse, "To the praise of the glory of his grace, wherein he hath made us accepted in the beloved" (Ephesians 1:6).

Since the self-centered life is the problem, it follows that its grip must be weakened — not strengthened. John the Baptist got hold of this truth when he made the statement in John 3:30, "He must increase, but I must decrease."

The apostle Paul states this principle succinctly in II Corinthians 12:9,10b: "And he said unto me, My grace is sufficient for thee: for my strength is made perfect in weakness. Most gladly therefore will I rather glory in my infirmities, that the power of Christ may rest upon me . . . for when I am weak, then am I strong." Since our weakness makes way for His strength, it follows that our weakness is the vehicle for manifesting His power. The ultimate in weakness is death, and this is precisely the manner in which Christ's life and power are unleashed. The verse which best depicts this vital spiritual principle is Galatians 2:20: "I am [have been] crucified with Christ: nevertheless I live; yet not I, but Christ liveth in me: and the life which I now live in the flesh I live by the faith of [or in] the Son of God, who loved me, and gave himself for me."

It is the author's prayer that this death-life principle may become operative in the life of the reader so that the Lord Jesus Christ may be glorified.

# Rejection: A Family Thing

# 1

A PSYCHOLOGICAL DISTURBANCE OF EPIDEMIC PROPORTIONS

In working with persons who have mental and emotional disturbances there is one trait which pervades most, if not all, of those seen in the counseling office. This trait is characterized by an impaired ability to give or receive love and is usually traceable to a person's childhood and parents who had the same problem. Although there may have been a type of love in the home, a child sensed some degree of overt or covert rejection — hence, the categorization of symptoms which follow could be subsumed under the heading, the Rejection Syndrome.

## OVERT REJECTION

Overt rejection is defined as open or obvious behavior which conveys the message to a child that he is unwanted or unloved. Covert rejection takes place in subtle ways which many times are not intended by a parent. The death of a parent, for example, may be perceived by a child as rejection. Over-protection also tends to prevent a child from developing normally. Emotionally, if not intellectually, he may conclude that he is not an adequate person. This leaves him no rational manner in which to cope with his sense of inadequacy. The mind and emotions being at variance with one another, the stage is set for emotional conflict and the resulting neurotic behavior. Many persons come from a background of extensive psychotherapy and still do not understand the rejection in their childhoods and its impact on their present intrapersonal and interpersonal relationships.

There are needs in a person's development from childhood onward which may be cataloged under the headings of physiological, psychological and spiritual. There is general consensus as to the physiological needs so these will not be discussed. However, there is much controversy as to the psychological and spiritual needs and the manner in which these may be met. The purpose of this chapter is to delineate the effects on the personality when love is lacking in the home or when the love is there but is not expressed in a manner which is meaningful to the child.

There are many reasons why parents reject their children, but the basic and ultimate reason is selfishness which stems from their own experiences of rejection. This manifests itself in many ways. One of the most common is that of parents who wanted no children. Since children interfere with a self-centered life style, their presence is a constant irritation and limitation. So the resulting frustration and hostility is vented upon these children. Rarely can the parents point out personality traits in the children which are sufficient to warrant rejection and many such parents do not understand why they reject their children. In fact, many would even deny that they do reject them. Even in the case of overt rejection there is love shown at times when the person has nothing pressing that he really wants to do and desires a plaything much as he would a pet.

The rejection may take the form of telling a child that he

14

was unwanted or that the parent wishes the child had never been born, both of which are overt rejection. Also, it may be a "cold war" approach where little or no affection is shown either because a parent finds it impossible to express affection or does not spend enough time in the home to do so. In the latter, a parent may be away from home constantly, participating in various activities — including church work. Many ministers and lay workers fall into this category since it is acceptable and considered commendable to be "about the Father's business." In many cases they should be about the business of being a father — or mother. A large percentage of those doing church work or even soul winning may be doing so because they dislike themselves so much they try to compensate by doing "good works," leaving no time to stay home and enjoy their families.

Many of those busily engaged in church work have deep, unresolved problems. Often these people lack a feeling of acceptance, and therefore their motives in church work are not altogether altruistic. They are really seeking acceptance from those they "help." These persons usually feel that they are not acceptable to God when they are not busy "serving the Lord." Thus, the more they "serve" to meet their own needs while ostensibly ministering to others, the more they reject their families. As their children begin to act-out and cause problems by their behavior, the parent's guilt could cause them to redouble their efforts and get involved in community programs to combat delinquency. Thus, the spiral goes from personal involvement or escape, to church involvement, to community or even political activities with each step resulting in greater estrangement from the children and increased guilt.

The whole behavior pattern is self-defeating. Since the person goes out to buy acceptance from others by performing services for them, his time is consumed and he has no time to love his wife (which he sees as bringing no adequate return for time invested) nor to love his children (who are a threat rather than a joy). Since he knows he is defaulting on his responsibilities at home he soon reaches the point of diminishing returns as the acceptance he receives outside is not sufficient to offset the guilt incurred at home. Thus, the latter condition is worse than the first. He has tried all known remedies — escaping in television, sleep, tranquilizers, alcohol, work or compulsive service in church — all to no avail. The logical next step is to make the rejection of the family final and legal through divorce and attempting to find happiness through another mate only to repeat the same process in another family.

The downward spiral takes less time in the second family since the spectre of guilt from copping out on past responsibility is the foundation for the second marriage. Children of the second mate are a reminder of the rejected children in the first marriage and present a constant threat so they are likewise rejected. This drives a wedge between the person and the new mate, and the conflict necessitates finding an escape again. In many cases the remarriage closes the door on some of the avenues of escape in church work, so the person begins to go the way of the world. This sin, added to his previous load of guilt, becomes too much to bear. His patterns of experiencing rejection and rejecting others sometimes results in the heightened rejection of himself which, when carried to the ultimate, is suicide.

The manner in which a parent rejects his children is sometimes inversely proportional to the manner in which he himself was rejected, although he often treats them just as he was treated. For instance, the child abuser is more often than not a former abused child himself. The data bear out that parenting techniques are largely learned from one's own parents. When a person's parents have been overly strict with him, he will usually be very rigid, but he may compensate in his children by being very lenient with them. If the children do not have sufficient guidelines to know where they stand, they can easily feel that the parents do not love them enough to care where they are or what they do. If their safety is not a significant aspect of their parent's concern, they can feel neglected and rejected. Many teenagers who are delinquent enjoy the freedom initially but then grow to resent their parents because they do not establish limits and discipline them when the boundaries are exceeded. Thus, uncontrolled freedom is a subtle or covert form of rejection.

The opposite of this is the parent who had lenient parents and vows in his heart that his children will have proper guidance. His "guidance" becomes so strict that the child reads it as being without love, understanding and compassion. Consequently, he experiences rejection. The overbearing parent may create fear on the part of the child rather than security. Ephesians 6:4 and Colossians 3:21 admonish the father not to provoke his children to wrath lest they become embittered or discouraged. Fathers who are too demanding and punish their children out of hostility rather than love put the children in a "no win" position. The child eventually gets the idea he can do nothing right and, consequently, loses all motivation and becomes discouraged.

The type of rejection sometimes manifested in succeeding generations is much like English on a cue ball — it reverses itself each time it hits the rail of the table. As seen above, a person who has strict parents may be more lenient with his children; and the person who had lenient parents may bear down on his children.

The more overt types of rejection are rather easily discerned by parent and child alike. The parent who deserts his family has obviously rejected his children. Rejection is also evident when a parent tells a child, "I wish you had never been born," or, "If the war had not taken place you wouldn't be here." If a child is born long after the other children and is made to feel that he is a mistake or accident or is told that the parents wanted the opposite sex he will very likely suffer from overt rejection. The child who is mentally retarded or otherwise handicapped may be openly rejected by his parents and by his peers.

## COVERT REJECTION

The foregoing rejections are recognized by almost everyone — those doing the rejecting, those experiencing the rejection and those observing the rejection. A person who knows he has been rejected usually understands, at least to a limited degree, why he behaves as he does toward his parents, others and himself. In the more subtle forms of rejection, neither the parents, the child nor the average observer recognizes that it is taking place.

Covert rejection commonly takes the form of over-protection or over-indulgence. An example of this is a lady who had "wonderful Christian parents who loved her so much they did everything for her." She was born long after the remainder of the family, so it is unlikely that she was planned. Much of the "love" shown her could well have been to mask the guilt feelings of the parents who may not have wanted her in the first place. Everything was done for her, so she was not allowed to be a person. Since she was not accepted as a person, this amounted to rejection as a person. Therefore, the parents had unknowingly "loved her to death;" they had actually destroyed her. As a result, she searched for love outside the home and became pregnant in her mid-teens and forced into premature marriage. True to pattern, she reversed the form of rejection and slapped her baby in the crib when he was about a month old. She could not embrace the child and communicate love when he was almost school age. She had been through psychotherapy for several mental and emotional problems prior to entering into Spirituotherapy, but had not been shown that she was a classic picture of total rejection. That is why she had no understanding of her feelings of inferiority and inadequacy.

A similar case was a man who was also the youngest in the family and was protected from doing the most menial chores. As a result, he did not develop any ability to perform routine maintenance tasks and was totally frustrated when attempting to use tools to do building or repair work. The frustration would very rapidly move into violent hostility toward anyone or anything which happened to be nearby. His mother continually assured him of her love while his father sat mutely by. He had a feeling of closeness to his father and bitter resentment toward his mother which he had never verbalized. This "love" which his mother expressed angered him, and he had no name for the feeling toward his father. He was totally confused as to a definition of love which had any meaning whatever.

This son could not receive love because he didn't recognize it, and he couldn't give what he didn't possess. Therefore, he rejected his parents and retreated into intellectual pursuits where he could excel by using no more complicated a tool than a pencil or calculator. Subsequently, in his marriage he refused to perform tasks around the home and continued his withdrawal which necessitated the rejection of his wife and children. His mounting hostility sometimes resulted in physical damage to property and verbal abuse to his wife when she expressed her love to him. Although he had never verbalized it nor understood it, his inner feeling was that his wife was a phony when she said "I love you," since this had been his attitude toward his mother's expression of love. After his father's death there was an aching void as he realized this feeling for his father had been unexpressed love. This thorough rejection had been so subtle that he could not recognize it and understand the effect it had on his attitude toward himself and his interpersonal relationships.

Another subtle or covert type of rejection is withdrawing love when performance is not up to the expected standard.

And, too frequently, when the child finally attains the standard, the standard is raised. He can seldom, if ever, "measure up." When he does "measure up" he is accepted for what he *does* — not for what he *is*; this means his performance is accepted but he, himself, is rejected.

It should again be emphasized that much rejection is probably not recognized as such by those doing it nor are they aware of how their behavior is affecting the offended person. Even in many cases of overt rejection the person does not recognize it as such. So often the rejection is unintentional and much guilt is suffered as a person comes to grips with the fact that he has overtly or covertly rejected a child — perhaps all the children. Many times a person will justify this rejection as a reaction to their unruly behavior, without recognizing that they are merely playing the role they have been taught: You have rejected me, so I will reject you.

Much rejection takes place because parents have such emotional and mental turmoil that they are barely able to maintain their own sanity, much less provide a stable, loving and accepting environment for their children. Over and over the counselor hears that a closer relationship has been established with the parents after the children have reached adulthood and begin to understand that it was not a personal rejection but the only behavior the parents could manifest while attempting to cope with their own internal and external pressures.

## ILLUSTRATION OF OVERPROTECTION

For many, it is difficult to grasp hold of the fact that over-protecting a child or over-indulging him is a rejection of him as a person. An illustration involving an animal sometimes serves to drive this point home.

Let the reader assume that he is desirous of having a pet and, in walking around a forest, comes upon a fox pup. He is cute and cuddly and the decision is made to domesticate him and train him as a family pet. He is taken to the place of residence, and the best of quarters are provided for his use. These might consist of a gigantic pen or play area, a beautiful and spacious fox house, a watering device he can depress with his nose, and everything else a fox's heart could desire along with some he would never dream possible. The stage is now set for all of his physical needs to be amply met. In addition, you give unstintingly of your time and devotion in play and training so that the growing fox has no lack of love and attention. In fact, he probably thinks he is a "people" since he has never seen a fox, and his pen is not lined with mirrors.

He has the best of food, plenty of exercise and all that makes for the epitome of physical conditioning. Thus, he is a perfect specimen of foxhood and might possibly take a grand prize in the local fox show. To all outward appearances, there could be no point in which he would fall short.

This "love affair" continues until the fox is fully grown at 18 - 21 months at which time you are now convinced that it is unfair to keep him penned up for the rest of his life. Although it tears your heart out to part with him, on his 21-month's birthday you greet him: "Well, Foxy, today you are an adult fox, so in all fairness I must give you your freedom. I have loved you and have done everything I knew to do for you, and now you are ready to try your hand (or paw) at living the life of an adult fox."

With this grand announcement you pick him up and take him to the same place you found him, kiss him on the nose, wish him the best of luck in his adult life and leave him to an environment perfectly suited to the needs of a fox.

Now, let's look in on him the next morning. He awakens and stretches and looks around for the bowl of nicely chopped meat and finds it strangely missing. Also, he is thirsty and looks for the mechanism to nudge with his nose to get some water, all to no avail. Later on, he sees a small four-legged critter amble by, but he doesn't know this is food because he has always had it conveniently prepared for him without his effort in killing it. As his hunger intensifies and he begins to weaken, a larger four-legged critter approaches which knows that he (beloved Foxy) *is* food! Since Foxy has neither learned the principles of fight or flight, he is very likely to *become* a meal instead of *receiving* one. The predator which he confronts has grown up under conditions suitable for the development of his innate abilities as a member of the animal kingdom, Foxy is no match for him.

The fox hadn't lacked for love, yet the circumstances and environment in which the love was received were actually detrimental. He was loved, accepted, and comfortable in his role as a pet but totally unprepared to meet the decisions and exigencies of adult life. Since he was not accepted in his proper role as a fox, he was totally rejected *as a fox*. In other words he was *rejected with love!*

In like manner, a child who is not taught or allowed to be a person and given the proper environment to develop as a person is rejected as a person. He grows up physically, but his emotional and, perhaps, intellectual development is stunted so that he is totally unprepared to assume adult responsibilities. However, he looks great on the outside; and when he flubs it as a teenager or adult and exhibits childish or juvenile behavior, he is told to "Snap out of it" or "Grow up and quit acting so immature and irresponsible." He may be so emotionally crippled that he finds it impossible to function in an adult role.

Those around him do not appreciate his need for crutches. A person who is missing a leg obviously needs crutches, and a person with cancer gets the empathy and understanding of those close to him. A person who has been crippled emotionally may suffer as much, or more, and those around cannot enter into his pain or help him bear his burden. In fact, they are more prone to deny his need of help to grow and mature emotionally and may demand of him performance beyond his capability. In doing so they have further rejected him and forced him to rely on his "crutches" which may be less acceptable to them than his inadequate performance as a person.

Alcohol is a very frequent "crutch" that an emotionally imm•ture person leans upon. The longer he depends upon it the less effective it becomes until he is in the throes of alcoholism. His deterioration under the enslavement of alcoholism frequently eventuates in a divorce and loss of family which is a further rejection.

If he doesn't get adequate help at this point, he may drift out of his employment and toward skid row where he rejects and is rejected by society. Here, he commits suicide by degrees with the bottle. Some braver souls may end their lives suddenly and avoid the long, drawn out procedure.

Those who have had the good fortune to grow up in an environment where they could mature emotionally and intellectually stand idly by and cluck their tongues at such an "immature and irresponsible" person. They bemoan the fact that he chooses to waste his life in such a manner when he has a great personality and everyone likes him and he has a good education and he has everything going for him. Why doesn't he shape up and take advantage of all his multitudinous opportunities?

This story could be recounted in various dimensions from all walks of life but the salient points continue to be repeated in lives and families throughout the world. Many a man who has been over-protected and thus rejected in his developmental stages marries and his wife takes the dominant role and continues the rejection. First, his mother (and/or father) would not let him grow up; then his wife takes up where Mom left off, usually being unaware of what she is doing. As the years pass, he continues to avoid facing the results of his behavior with the "help" of his wife, until that situation presents itself where she is unable to bail him out. At this point he is left alone (rejected) to negotiate a course for which he is ill-prepared; and when he falls flat on his face those who have been instrumental in destroying him as a person are too often the first to put him down for his failure.

And, to add insult to injury, there are always those who want to throw away his crutches before he has matured internally to the point that he can "walk alone." When a person has his crutches removed before his leg is healed, he is likely to fall on his face! The same is true of the emotional cripple. The person needs to learn that there is One within, or who can come within — the Lord Jesus Christ — upon whom he can depend for support which makes crutches unnecessary. Christ has become his life so that he will *always* have His support and acceptance and will never be rejected (Hebrews 13:5,6).

The child whose parent or parents have died may perceive parental death as rejection. Unless the parent committed suicide, he had no choice in the matter, but he is not present to show the child love. If a boy's mother dies and leaves him, he may find it very difficult ever to trust women. It was so painful to lose his mother that he may consciously or unconsciously vow, "I'll never let another woman get that close to me again!" Unless his wife understands this she can never get a handle on his behavior toward her and, perhaps, their children.

One lady had a stepdaughter who was 17 and had not yet forgiven her mother for dying when she was 13.

Children involved in a divorce are very apt to suffer rejection. They may have related most closely to the parent who was ejected from the home, and that parent might still be the most capable of communicating love to the children. However, when the parent is not available in the home to demonstrate love and affection, the children can perceive it as rejection.

Since a child can read the absence of a parent as rejection, the child who has been adopted has automatically experienced rejection by his natural parents. All too frequently, the adoptive parents are so delighted at having finally received a child that they smother or over-indulge the child, and he experiences another form of rejection.

An "only child" is frequently spoiled or over-protected since the parents have too much time (and perhaps money) to lavish upon him. Since they do not have to share their time with other children, they are ever present to make decisions for the child or to do for him things that he is perfectly capable of doing himself. In so doing they are tacitly saying, "You are too stupid to do it so I will do it for you." When this message is communicated to a child in words or actions over a period of time, he finally gets the message that he is inferior and feels that he can not do anything well.

Children who have not matured in social responsibilities are frequently told by exasperated parents, "You'll never amount to anything!" It is not difficult to see how inferiority feelings can stem from such statements.

# The Aftermath of Rejection

The foregoing presents some causes and effects regarding the development of rejective behavior on the part of the parent and the reaction of the child in a more general manner. Now, let's turn to some more specific attitudes and feelings engendered within the person by rejection or lack of responsible love.

## REJECTION AND THE INDIVIDUAL

The person who has experienced rejection gets the feeling, which he may not be able to express, that he is unwanted. If he feels unwanted, then he naturally feels worthless or unnecessary. If he feels unworthy of his parent's love, he also feels inferior. If he feels unworthy and inferior, he must be a burden to his parents and, hence, must be the cause of many of their problems. This induces guilt which becomes a way of life, and he generally feels guilty for existing and almost apologizes for living.

This is the genesis of much false or imaginary guilt. Since

27

his parents are the source of his feelings of worthlessness, inferiority and guilt, it is logical that he doubts the acceptance and love on the part of others who have less reason to love him. He tends to be guarded and defensive in all his interpersonal relationships and rarely, if ever, reveals himself to others or develops close personal relationships. He puts on a front to appear the way he thinks others want him to be and says what they want to hear so that he will be acceptable or accepted. Frequently he says "yes" when he means "no" and vice versa. Since his parents have rejected him, he finds himself unacceptable and proceeds to reject himself. He finds nothing good about himself in his intelligence, his appearance nor his behavior. It is second nature for him to find fault with himself and to condemn himself. When he is wronged by others, he cannot express anger or hostility because he might lose what meager acceptance he has gained. He has no choice but to turn the hostility inward in self-condemnation. This eventuates in depression and anxiety.

All his life decisions must be made from a stance of weakness which prevents his entering into relationships or vocations that will maximize his potential since he feels he *has* little, if any, potential. His rejection by parents has resulted in his rejection of himself and he is programmed to cause others to reject him.

Since this kind of person does not know how to handle love and acceptance, those who do accept him must somehow be turned off so they will finally reject him and fit the pattern with which he can cope. In other words, he rejects them before they have a chance to reject him. When they reciprocate, it proves that they reject him just as everyone else has. If anything good is said about him, he must instantly find something wrong since the statement does not agree with the way he feels about himself. When others accept him as he is, or at least as he appears to them, it is meaningless to him because he feels they would not accept him if they knew how he really felt.

This person feels that others thoroughly reject him, and he has rejected himself. Therefore, he rejects anything he has done or any extension of himself, which includes his children. As stated earlier, the form of rejection toward his children may be opposite to that accorded him by his parents. His lack of worthiness makes him feel unacceptable to God as well as to men, and he frequently casts God in the role of a rejecting father. Having difficulty attaining acceptance on a human level, it is only natural that he would feel unacceptable to God. Such persons who have received Christ as Lord and Savior still find it difficult to believe that God loves them unconditionally. They believe that the Bible is God's Word and that it expresses His love for them, and yet they can't relax from their own works or efforts and realize His love and acceptance at an experiential level. It seems to them that prayers of others are answered but not their own. The lack of acceptance on a human or psychological basis carries over into the spiritual realm. Not feeling accepted by others, they do not feel accepted by God. Their emotions are almost always at variance with reality. As a result, they feel unworthy and unsaved even though they know their salvation is assured biblically.

## FEELINGS VS. KNOWLEDGE

The disagreement between intellect and emotion in many cases derives from the fact that the person as a child was not permitted to do many things he knew intellectually he could do. For example, a teenager may know intellectually that he can learn to drive a car because others his age are capable of such a task. However, if he is never permitted to get behind the wheel of a car, he might *feel* that he could never learn to drive. If he is never able at the proper time to verify in experience what he knows intellectually, he will continue to

29

have a discrepancy between what he *knows* to be true and what he *feels* to be true. And his feelings will seem to be more real, so he conducts his life on the basis of the feelings rather than truth. This results in distorting reality to agree with emotions. This is known in psychological circles as neurosis. It follows that those who do not feel the same way will see their behavior as being illogical.

Many parents of unwanted children attempt to convince their children (and themselves) that they do love them. Since a child can not be fooled by the phony expressions of "love" by the parents, he is faced with a double message. "I love you" is the message in words to his mind but "I hate you" is the message received by his emotions. Since the rejection is subtle, the child reacts to it without knowing what it is. This is the classic setup for the beginning stages of schizophrenia — a conflicting message to the mind and the emotions. He *knows* one thing with his mind and *feels* another with his emotions. This puts him in a double bind since the two messages cannot be reconciled. When it is no longer possible to tolerate the conflict, a retreat from reality occurs, known as a psychotic break. After the break, the mind and emotions "do their own thing" with little or no cooperation. Thus, a person might laugh at news of a family tragedy or in other ways respond inappropriately to communication.

Interpersonal relationships are grossly hampered by such conditions. When one person relates to a situation as it is and another as he *feels* it is, it is very difficult, if not impossible, to arrive at a common conclusion. Thus, communication cannot be conducted on a rational basis. Relationships also break down unless the person who is objective can tolerate the illogical behavior without extreme frustration.

## PSYCHOLOGICAL DISTURBANCES

Rejection is one of the prime causes of psychological disturbances. It is of utmost importance to understand this behavior as well as the means for resolution of the symptomatology. The antidote to rejection is acceptance, but this must take place on a supernatural level if the basic problem is to be resolved. The response to God's love and acceptance must first be initiated in the will or volition by faith, since neither mind nor emotions are functioning in a manner consistent with reality. Although the emotional and mental symptoms are a result of unfortunate experiences with parents and others, the basic problem is self or flesh in control of the life.

All mental and emotional aberrations, aside from malfunctioning organs, glands, etc., are a function of the self-life. The manner in which self responds to persons and situations has been pre-determined during the developmental stages of life. The emotions are shaped (or bent out of shape) by an environment of rejection. Such a person, of course, has a poor self-image. However, it makes no difference how much self is improved, it is still *self!* It can be trained through therapy or self-help programs of various kinds, and this may be of some value in alleviating symptoms. But God's answer is not to make self stronger, but weaker to the point of "death" — the death that is the reckoning of our co-crucifixion or union with Christ. Once this is an appropriated reality, and Christ has become the life, His life is not affected by the rejective behavior of parents or others. The person then is set free from the bondage of defeat and illogical behavior to be governed from within by the One who is perfectly adjusted. This Person, the Lord Jesus Christ, is not only in touch with reality, *He is Himself Reality* (John 1:1-4, 14; Colossians 1:15-17) — the Way, the Truth, and the Life (John 14:6).

Growing up in an atmosphere of rejection, programs one for rejection. And when he finds himself in a situation where he is not rejected, he somehow sets it up so he will be rejected. Then he knows how to conduct himself. He is much like a person who has been in a prison cell (read Psalm 142) for years and hates it but knows every inch of the place. After a while, his prison cell becomes his protection or security. He can respond to any situation except freedom! In time, the prospect of freedom becomes his greatest fear. The inmate might refuse a pardon and spend his life in prison rather than accept the responsibility that comes with freedom. In like manner, many who have learned to cope with their prison of psychological disturbances cannot tolerate the idea of freedom from these enslaving patterns. In John 5:6 the Lord Jesus asked a man who had been imprisoned by physical handicaps, "Wilt thou be made whole?" On the surface this sounds like an idiotic question; one would think that any person who had been crippled for 38 years would jump at the opportunity to be healed. But what was involved for the cripple? He had a very legitimate excuse to cop out on responsibility — his physical disadvantage. It was necessary for others to support him and he developed greater and greater dependency. If he is healed, he must not only take the responsibility for his own support but also begin to help other unfortunates, who may be unable to help themselves. Jumping from total dependence to a state of independence in one giant step can be a frightening proposition.

Let's look at the cripple's response to Christ's question, "Do you want to be healed?" As you perhaps know it was only the first to get into the water after it had been "troubled" by the angel who was healed of "whatsoever disease he had." His reply to Jesus was that he had no man to help him into the water and, as a result, another always got in before him. Could it not have been merely a lack of faith on his part? If he were truly convinced that healing would take place, he could have lain on the edge and fallen into the pool; then it would have been a simple matter to swim out after being healed. It is always easier to lay the blame on others

32

than to admit our weak faith in God's "exceeding great and precious promises" (II Peter 1:4).

In counseling there are those who cannot honestly say that they want to be healed. They know they cannot cope with the freedom, and they have yet to understand that the One who sets them free will also be their wisdom and strength to handle the new-found freedom (Philippians 1:6).

## REJECTION IN MARRIAGE

Up to this point we have considered rejection of children and the fact that offspring so treated are very likely to reject their children. In addition, there are far-reaching effects in other interpersonal relationships and endeavors on the part of the person who has been rejected.

One of the most obvious relationships negatively affected by the results of rejection is the marital relationship. The person who has experienced rejection does not know how to give or receive love and has never learned basic trust. In addition, inferiority feelings prevent participation in some routine activities: attempting tasks which might result in failure, enjoyment of leisure time, setting long-range goals, and a myriad of other disabling behaviors. A well-adjusted mate attempting to cope with the above is at a disadvantage since he usually cannot understand the neurotic behavior, much less be empathic with his mate. With troubled marriages it is frequently found that a person who has experienced rejection has married another who comes from a similar background. Such people apply all their skills and knowledge in a pattern of mutual rejection. Their marriage is an ironic sort of blessing since they only destroy one union.

The person who has had a pattern of rejection from childhood will often read rejection into a situation or conversation where none exists. And, whether or not the rejection is actual, if he reads rejection into the conversation or circumstances, it opens up old rejection wounds which

33

amplify many times the supposed or actual rejection. The same statements or set of conditions where rejection actually existed might go completely unnoticed by a person not previously programmed for rejection. The person with old rejection wounds, on the other hand, may be completely devastated by merely being slighted in some particular.

Some couples try counseling with pastors, marriage counselors, psychologists or psychiatrists before winding up in the divorce courts. One man came in for counseling who had tried to touch every base in seeking help. He first visited an evangelical physician to inquire where solid Christian counseling help could be secured. With his wife willing to cooperate, they were referred to a psychiatrist who professed to be a Christian. After three interviews, he told the husband that his wife didn't want him so he might as well forget it. He paid around $150 for this information which was hardly news to him. Neither of them received any help with the personal problems which had caused the rift in the relationship. By the time he came for Spirituotherapy his wife refused to cooperate until after the divorce was final. After all, she had already tried "Christian" counseling!

Unless the damage to the emotions is rectified by the Spirit of God there is little use in working on the symptoms of the impaired relationship. The fact that a person is physically adult does not mean that his emotions have kept pace. An adult can be an intellectual genius and an emotional moron. Trying to live with a person possessing this combination of traits can be a very frustrating experience!

It is not at all unusual for someone to have undergone psychotherapy for months or even years and never have had uncovered the subtle rejection he had experienced and its deleterious effects on his opinion of himself, his emotional makeup and interpersonal relationships.

A common behavior manifested by those who have been severely rejected is that of clinging like a leech to a person who gives him the love which he has been seeking. When he finally finds someone who loves and accepts him, he monopolizes the person's time and is extremely jealous of any time the person spends with others. The demands on the person's time become so great that it becomes impossible to meet them. Any attempt to reduce the time consumed is taken as rejection and the only other alternative is to terminate the relationship which proves in the person's mind that all relationships eventually end in rejection.

What the rejected person doesn't realize is that he has not permitted his new-found friend the right to be a person and make free choices about the use of his time. In so doing he has rejected the one loving and befriending him and has unwittingly set the other person up to reject him.

On the other extreme, if the friend is able to weather the negativism, scorn, intolerance, and rejection and continue to show unconditional love, the person will cease his offensive and back off. It is almost like a dog chasing a car. If he ever caught it, he wouldn't know what to do with it! When a person has never had love, he doesn't know what to do with it when he gets it. Therefore, he finds some way to get the loving person to reject him so he will exhibit a behavior or emotion with which he can cope. Then, he blames the rejection on the other person and everything is back to *status quo*.

## REJECTION FROM INFANCY TO ADULTHOOD

A baby reacts to rejection even in the first few weeks of life. The mother who is nervous and afraid she cannot handle the new responsibility does not relax in her relationship with the baby and can pass the tension to the child, who in turn can manifest colic or other forms of irritable behavior.

As the rejected child grows he is usually either shy and quiet or hyperactive and difficult to manage. The former internalizes the rejection and he regards himself as being

35

unworthy of close relationships; the latter takes out his hostility on everything and everyone! The former is more introverted; the latter more extroverted. The introvert will try to prove to himself that he is capable or worthy while the extrovert tries to convince others that he excels in one way or another. The one shys away from deep relationships and the other drives away those who would be close. The introvert, because of cowardice, may be overly submissive and ingratiating to all who are in authority while the extrovert may openly flout all authority.

The teenager may be shy and withdrawn or rebellious and delinquent. The rebellious teenager who is delinquent is saying in effect, "I *will* be a person!" The withdrawn teenager is saying, "I don't *deserve* to be a person." Another alternative is the schizoid individual who withdraws and, in effect, says: "I don't need you; I'll be self-sufficient — now, you can't reject me anymore."

Many girls who have experienced rejection trade their bodies for a little acceptance only to realize later that their bodies were accepted while they, themselves, were rejected. Other young people marry at an early age in an effort to find love and acceptance which they failed to experience in their families. Some fall into homosexual relationships in adult life for the first time due to finding acceptance by such a person.

Many young people "date down" or establish relationships with persons who are below them in age, education, appearance, social status, etc., because they do not feel inferior in such relationships. Marriages established under such conditions seldom endure. If the person who marries beneath himself is able to surmount some of his feelings of inferiority with growth and maturity, the existing gap becomes an unbridgeable chasm. He may then choose to divorce his wife and marry someone he feels is more on his level.

The patterns of mutual rejection in marriage are many and

varied. The one who withdraws in adverse situations clams up and destroys communication. The one rejected who acts out and expresses his hostility further destroys the self-image of his mate and widens the chasm between them. Mutual trust can seldom be established since individuals who have experienced rejection often marry each other. The situation is almost as bad when a well-adjusted person marries a person from a background of rejection. It is exceedingly difficult for this type of person to have empathy for a mate who makes illogical assumptions and distorts statements and actions to make them fit with the way he *feels* things are. A rejected person may *know* he can trust his mate but *feels* as though he cannot. He may *know* that his mate is faithful but *feels* that an affair has taken or will take place; thus insecurity breeds jealousy.

When both mates have experienced rejection the situation is really wild! Each operates on what he *feels* to be true and the feelings of one are at variance to the feelings of the other. Therefore, each can *feel* that he is completely right and be very sincere and yet be at odds with the facts as they exist. The result is invariably mutual rejection.

As children are born into a home where mutual rejection is the order of the day they are caught in the crossfire. The parents can't accept themselves or each other and are too insecure to give acceptance and security to the children. The result, of course, is overt or covert rejection and the cycle has begun in the next generation.

## REJECTION AMONG SIBLINGS

In some cases where the children are accepted and treated equally by the parents there is rivalry among the children (or siblings) that results in the feeling of rejection by the one whose achievements are not on the par with another. Also, complicated patterns of rejection among siblings can result from the rejection train started by the parents.

37

A case comes to mind where the younger child was openly rejected by the father and a middle child was openly favored by him. The oldest child strongly identified with the youngest and felt her father rejected her because of it. The middle child experienced rejection by the other children because of the father's favoritism. Thus, the entire family was caught up in rejection in one form or another. It threatened to decimate the family until both father and mother appropriated their acceptance in Christ.

## REJECTION IN THE SCHOOL

Another area of life in which the rejection syndrome has devastating effects is education. In cases where open rejection is accompanied by a broken home, a series of different parents, etc., the child may have no stabilizing influence whatever. He not only has no help with his studies in the home, but he very quickly loses any motivation to learn in the classroom. Equipped with a poor self-image and no encouragement in an unfavorable environment, he may quickly fall behind in his work and the grade level in which he should be able to perform. If he is fortunate enough to be in a school which is able to diagnose his situation and give him help, it will almost always be in the areas of psychological and learning problems. Although there is no doubt that these exist, these are still only symptomatic in nature. He probably will not have any facility at learning until his emotional state is remedied. The remedy offered is usually not spiritual and has the effect of strengthening self, thus deferring any chance of the child getting the type of help he really needs.

It is realized that a teacher in a public school system is not free to give the needed spiritual help even if qualified to do so. At this juncture there is no alternative to the exclusive use of psychological and educational techniques.

Although the foregoing are extreme cases, there are

multiplied thousands who fit these descriptions in some particular. Even the less extreme cases fall into the category of underachieving. The public education system leaves much to be desired since the spiritual answer cannot be freely given. Most Christian schools do not have sufficient funds or personnel for adequate diagnosis and treatment in the emotional and learning areas. Most certainly, the schools fall short of giving adequate spiritual help to resolve deep emotional problems.

Much prayer is needed that God will supply the funds and personnel to pioneer an approach to education which is Christ-centered and can be taught to classroom teachers.

## SUMMARY AND EXAMPLES

Since the ways in which a child may be overtly rejected are easily understood, it is pointless to rehash the obvious. Accordingly, the following summary deals with some of the ways by which a child may experience covert rejection and the resulting damage within the person and to his interpersonal relationships. As previously stated, the results of rejection are much the same, whether due to overt or covert rejection.

### Variations of Covert Rejection

1) *Over-protection* — The parents may love the child so much that they do *everything* for him. They love the child enough to do anything for him *except* to let him become a person. When by their over-protectiveness they do not let him *become* a person he has been subtly rejected *as* a person.

Even though destroyed inwardly, the teenager may make a valiant attempt to become a person through open rebellion or he may turn inward and withdraw from the scene of action. In other words, he either "acts out" or "acts in." To complete the sad picture, the person so over-protected and rejected frequently marries a pillar of strength who takes up where the parents left off. The subtle rejection continues until the pillar of strength weakens and overtly rejects the mate through divorce.

2) *Death of parents*

Some parents have no better judgment than to "cop out" and die and leave a defenseless child an orphan! Barring suicide, the parent has no choice in the matter; but the child at an early age has no conception of this. All he knows is that he is alone and the parent(s) left him. He perceives rejection emotionally whether or not he ever understands it intellectually. He may consciously or unconsciously have the attitude that no one will ever get close enough to hurt him again in this way. The result? He rejects them before they get a chance to reject him. By keeping up his barrier, he can not get hurt; however, there is the corollary truth that he can't be loved either. He keeps out friend and foe alike rather than run the risk of loving and losing.

The adopted person, by definition, has been rejected or he would still be with his natural parents. To make matters worse, he may be with adoptive parents who waited years for a child and just "love him to death." He jumps out of the frying pan into the fire — from one subtle form of rejection to another!

3) *Wrong Sex*

Though not overtly rejected, a child may sense that his parents really wanted the opposite sex and that they are "extra nice" so he won't find it out.

4) *"Change of life" baby*

Very few parents plan children after their family is practically grown and they (the parents) are nearing middle age. They may "protest too much" to prove to the child that he really is loved and wanted.

5) *Broken home*

The parent who leaves the home may be the one to whom the child relates best in meeting his love needs. The child may be too young to understand why this parent can't live with him or spend uninterrupted time with him. To make matters worse, the parent with whom he lives may in subtle, or not so subtle, ways educate him to hate the one he loves most and convince him that the absentee parent didn't love him at all. Thus, he may be alienated or estranged from both parents and find the world an intolerable place in which to live.

6) *Suicide*

The parent who suicides not only hands the child the epitome of rejection but frequently leaves the child with a guilt complex for having caused it.

7) *Death in Childbirth*

Some children receive the message in various ways from

their fathers that they were the cause of their mother's death. By the time the child is able to reason the situation out, the emotional damage has already been done.

8) *Invidious comparison with siblings*

Parents, peers, and/or teachers may knowingly or unknowingly force a child to compete with another sibling for acceptance in a particular arena. Failure to succeed spells rejection in the mind of the child, if not on the part of others.

9) *Handicaps*

A handicapped child may sense that the parent(s) are not able to accept the handicap or the child so afflicted. In other cases the parents accept the child completely and the rejection takes place on the school ground.

10) *Conditional love*

A child who is loved because he performs according to criteria set by his parents is accepted only on the basis of performance. Hence, he is rejected even when he is accepted! He is "accepted" for what he *does*, not for what he *is*.

## INTRAPERSONAL EFFECTS OF REJECTION

The emotional damage that lies in the wake of rejection is much the same whether it stems back to overt or covert forms of rejection. When the situation without and within becomes intolerable and no avenue is open to resolve the conflict the mind may perform tricks to protect itself as well. Those symptoms which commonly pass for "mental illness" such as fantasy, or "going into one's head" as the young people put it, and most of the psychotic disorders are merely methods employed to enable a person to run away while standing still (or fidgeting).

Rather than deal to any extent with the variety of mental "copouts" available to a person, the following will be confined to the effects on the emotions. The emotional symptoms in the following discussion are not exhaustive nor are they treated thoroughly; these are typical and clearly describe the wide-ranging effects within the individual and some of the ways in which he is restricted in his ability to function as a person.

1) *Feelings of Worthlessness*

What could be more logical than that a person who is treated as having little or no worth should feel worthless? Such a person may feel that he is occupying someone else's space or breathing someone else's air! His actions and attitudes, if not his words frequently make it seem that he is apologizing for his own existence! Not only does he feel that his person is worthless but also any extension of himself is deserving of the same epithet; this includes his accomplishments in most areas and may even apply to his family. After all, if they had any smarts they wouldn't stay with anyone so worthless as he!

**Illustration:**

A lady fitting the above description made a food item which was highly complimented by her roommate. She became so angry she was almost violent! In her eyes the compliment was ridicule and a lie since nothing she did could ever be worthy of an adjective denoting excellence.

2) *Wishing he hadn't been born*

This statement is frequently heard in the counseling office. One lady remembers trying to find a way to be "unborn" at a very early age since her parents told her they didn't want her. Others who reject the idea of suicide but have found no viable alternative frequently express such a wish. Their parents wish they hadn't been born so the child or person is merely expressing his agreement.

3) *Feelings of Inferiority*

The so-called "inferiority complex" derives from the ingrained feelings of worthlessness or inferiority which have been accepted as fact by the individual. The logic runs, "I *feel* inferior; therefore, I must *be* inferior." Even though a

43

person has irrefutable evidence that he is average or superior in certain traits and/or endeavors to which he gives mental assent, he allows the feeling to override the fact and chooses to base many life actions on the feeling. A person may *feel* inferior and yet be the valedictorian of his class.

The writer has asked several women who were beautiful by the most severe standards what their reaction would be to the statement, "You are beautiful." The immediate retort comes back, "I am *not!*" Translated, I do not feel beautiful; therefore, I am not beautiful.

A person who has been told by words or actions that he is stupid, will never amount to anything, or can never do anything right repeatedly will eventually begin to feel that way.

4) *Inability to express feelings*

A person who feels he has no valid reason for being and hates himself doesn't dare express his true feelings. He may lose the acceptance he has bought by exchanging services (being what others want him to be) and others will probably hate him as much as he hates himself!

This is sometimes misread in marriage as a communication problem. However, most couples speak the same language; anything he says may be used against him and he will "lose face" with his mate.

He was probably "shushed" and put down from early childhood at any time he attempted to express his feelings. In addition to being afraid to express himself, he was never permitted to develop the skills of communication; at a later date the stakes are too high to attempt it.

5) *Depression*

For the severely rejected, depression is a way of life. The writer's homespun definition of depression is. an internal temper tantrum. The forms of depression and degree of severity are usually a function of the circumstances and support available.

6) *Emotional Insulation*

A person builds a wall around himself for protection but it works two ways; it not only keeps others out, but it also keeps him in! Communication is impaired since he throws a few words across his wall and the other person may do the same. Their walls clang together but they never touch! The price of safety is a type of self imposed isolation.

It is as though he were in a prison. He may hate it but he knows every inch of it. He may get to the place where his greatest fear is freedom. The "prison cell" eventually provides a neurotic type of security.

7) *Subjectivity*

Such a person is controlled to a great extent by his emotions; he may be said to "think with his feelings". An observer may find his behavior illogical and inexplicable since it is based on feelings rather than facts. A person who argues a point with him based on logic may become very frustrated when the reply comes back, "But I *feel* this is the way it is!"

8) *Introspection*

Looking inward to try and analyze the cause of failure or anticipated failure or for some mysterious sin which refuses to surface and be identified becomes a daily occupation (or pre-occupation). All known sins are confessed times without number to the point where the person thinks he is pious and doing God a favor by putting himself down! In a neurotic sort of way he gets even with himself. All the while he is going through these maneuvers his Father sees him as a believer "seated in heavenly places in Christ Jesus." (Ephesians 2:6).

9) *Perfectionism*

This frequently has its genesis in an ill-fated attempt to "make it" with one or both parents. "I'm doing everything just perfect, Mom and Dad; please love and accept me!" This is the rationale behind it but it never pays off. As soon as the goal is within sight the parents move the goal. As an adult he

45

has internalized the high standards and never reaches them; in turn, they are laid on his mate and children who likewise never "measure up" and are rejected on a poor-performance basis. He winds up doing exactly the same thing to his children for which he hated (or at least resented) his parents.

10) *Lack of self-discipline*

After having been told what, how and when to perform, it shouldn't be surprising that he has little or no skills in self-direction or in decision making.

11) *Irresponsibility*

Since he was never deemed worthy of responsibility, he never learned to assume it or discharge it. Fear of failure prevents attempting many tasks he really wants to do but is misread by others as slothfulness or stubbornness.

A person may accept the invitation to be on a church board or committee and never show up for a single meeting. Why? He wins two ways: he isn't rejected by the person who asks him, and he never shows up to be rejected by his failure to perform satisfactorily.

12) *Worries, doubts, fears*

These are ubiquitous and self-explanatory. A common catch-all name for the combination is anxiety. We ignore God's command to be anxious for nothing (Philippians 4:6) and worry about everything. If there is a respite from worry, the person worries because he isn't worrying!

13) *Self-condemnation*

Others have always put him down or condemned him so he learns the game well and every day is "beat up on self day."

14) *Self-hatred*

He feels he is totally justified and deserves the approbation of others for hating such a worm as he! Though the scripture enjoins us to love our neighbors as we love ourselves, many Christians never recognize this activity as sin. If such Christians loved their neighbors as they do themselves, their neighbors would be in mortal danger!

A lady who had a childhood of total rejection still sucked her thumb after being married and having children. Upon the inquiry as to whether she had confessed the sin of self-hatred, she replied that she had never recognized it as sin. She was shown that she had no more right, scripturally, to hate herself than to hate others. Confession and learning who she was in Christ resulted in freedom.

15) *Guilt*

The guilt feeling or false guilt is a concomitant of rejection. A person feels that he is causing any difficulty or conflict that arises as a child or is told that he is unwanted; he feels guilty for being there and grows up feeling guilty for being a person. He has a case of the "guilties" even when he is all "'fessed up". He may confess sin until he is blue in the face and answer multitudinous altar calls with no relief.

Another source of false guilt is that a person can't forgive himself even though God's Word has assured his forgiveness. In a manner of speaking such a person places himself on a higher plane than God; even though God has made good His provision of forgiveness, the person remains staunch in his unforgiving attitude toward himself. He is saying, in effect, "Father, my standards are higher than yours; I can not forgive me." The false guilt is in the emotions, hence the name "guilt feelings"; when the source, self in control of the life, is dealt with the symptoms in the emotions are readily resolved.

**Summary:**

The foregoing were caused by rejection on the part of others with the inevitable result that the person rejects himself. The ultimate in self-rejection is suicide — the epitome of self-centeredness!

## Interpersonal Effects of Rejection

The interpersonal effects of rejection are radiated in all

# REJECTION ILLUSTRATED

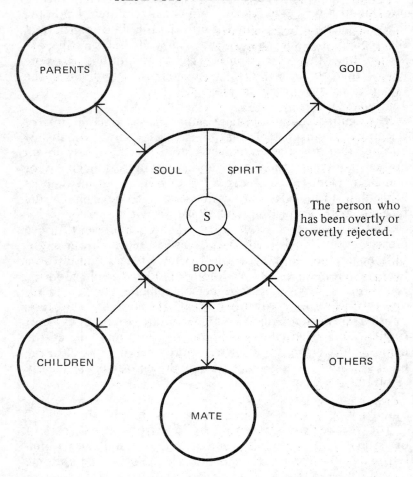

The person who has been overtly or covertly rejected.

*DIAGRAM 1*

*In all of the above relationships except with God, the person is rejected and reciprocates with rejection. He also rejects God, at least for a time, but never succeeds in getting God to reject him.*

directions — back to the parents and beyond them to God, out to the mate and others and downward to the children. A person may reject his children by treating them in the same manner that his parents treated him. Or, he may say, "I'm going to give my children that which I didn't have." How many parents have not vocalized this in reference to some facet of the child's life? The person who was battered as a child and hated his parents for it frequently batters his own children. The person who received no love may smother and overprotect his children and reject them in the opposite manner. Or, the person who suffered over-protection may insist that his child be independent almost from the cradle.

Some of the attitudes and reactions engendered by rejection follow:

1) *Toward parents and God*

There is resentment, if not hatred, for the emotional pain which has been suffered and bitterness may continue for a lifetime. The child or young person may "clam up" and refuse to communicate. By such refusal he is saying, in effect, "I refuse to let you in." He may not have the guts to act out so he withdraws. The braver soul acts out and we reap the results in an epidemic of teenage rebellion. As the rebellion mounts in intensity the parents protest:"How can they do this to *me* after all I've done for them; I've given them *everything!*" or "I've done everything for them!" Too many times, the parents have given everything but *themselves* and they have done everything for the child but to accept him *unconditionally* as a person.

The rebellion against the parents is frequently generalized to all in authority — teachers, civil authority, and sooner or later, God.

The overprotected person is often ambivalent toward his parents; he loves them for what they have done *for* him and hates them for what they have done *to* him. When the rejection has been covert, he doesn't understand how he could harbor hatred for such loving, wonderful parents. Thus, he hates himself all the more for being so despicable as to have unfounded hatred.

He learns to distrust his parents and finds it very difficult to trust anyone including God. He may *know* (intellectually) that he can trust God but *feels* that he can't. Since his feelings are in the ascendancy, whatever is felt is the governing factor. Since the parents and others are seen as rejecting and condemning, he sees God in much the same way; and his attitude may be summed up towards his parents and God, "You've rejected me so I will reject you."

2) *Toward mate and/or children*

Impaired ability to express feelings, positive or negative, applies to both spouse and children. Those times when feelings are freely expressed are usually when all control has been lost and the result is a net loss. When affection was not shown by the parents as the child grew up, the home he establishes is usually quite similar. When the mate can not absorb all of the hostility, the stage is set for conflict.

The children and mate are more tolerated than enjoyed. Much punishment of the children is done in a fit of anger to vent the parent's hostility. When the punishment is undeserved or is inordinate compared with the seriousness of the infraction of house rules, the child perceives it as rejection.

A parent may make one statement while in a rage such as "I wish you had never been born!" Even though it was under the stress of that particular situation, the child may always remember it. It might be a little more subtle; one person reported that his parents had told him, "If it hadn't been for the war you wouldn't be here!" The fact that he was an only child served to prove the point.

A child is put in a double bind when he hears the words, "I love you, I love you"; but with his emotions he picks up the feeling, "I hate you, I hate you!" This sets his mind and emotions at variance and he usually doesn't have the resources to reconcile the two conflicting messages. He may well adopt the attitude, "If this is love I don't need some!" When the mind and emotions function independently of each other the person could be described as psychotic.

All of the decisions may be made for the children in an over-protective home or the child may have practically no guidance. In the latter case he may well infer, "My parents do not love me enough to establish firm limits on my behavior." Both ends of the continuum are equally rejective.

As has been previously stated, the parent who has been abused as a child frequently resorts to the same treatment of his own children.

Refusal to communicate with spouse and/or children is rejective in that others are barred from sharing his life. "I refuse to let you in because you may hurt me as others have" or "You are not important enough for me to admit you to the inner recesses of my life." These are common attitudes which may not be understood nor expressed by those harboring them.

When the parent(s) spend most of their free time in the company of others, the child has every right to infer that other people are important but he isn't. Even the minister frequently falls prey to this. Every time Sister Jones has a sore toe the pastor must be there to comfort her, but little Johnny may never see Dad at one of his ball games; or Suzie may miss him at her recital. In passing, church members unthinkingly reject their pastor by not permitting him to be a person or father and demanding (tacitly) that he be at every church function and bedside.

When a child is told that he should be "seen and not heard," he is denied the right to be a person. This is one of the many ways in which he internalizes the message — "You can be a person when you grow up." By the time he grows up he doesn't know how to be a person since he has never been allowed the privilege. Once he is adolescent or grown the parents not infrequently ask the question, "Why don't you grow up? You are so immature". He has every right to ask in reply, "I'd love to; why don't you let me?"

His decision-making capability was not encouraged nor developed but he is usually put down for inappropriate decisions or for not acting at all. He is ill-equipped for life and marriage since marriage isn't for those who behave as children.

3) *Toward others*

The trait which pervades all others is the impaired ability to give and receive love. He can't accept love because of the fear that it may be withdrawn through choice or death, and he can't give that which he has never received or doesn't possess.

Although the search for love and acceptance has been a compelling urge, the attainment of the goal may be more frustrating than the quest. Those who have been severely rejected can handle anything but love. They are programmed to see rejection in everyone and everything. If it isn't there they will somehow bring it about so they will know how to conduct themselves. When a person sets about to love them in Christ no matter how much they try to turn it aside, the result would be comical if it weren't so tragic. When such a person finally capitulates to the love of Christ flowing through another person, he is well on his way to freedom. And it *has* to be the love of Christ since human love is insufficient to sustain continued rebuff over protracted periods of time. Too, only the love of Christ can draw a person, saved or unsaved, to appropriate his death and resurrection with Christ and thus be released from the ingrained effects of past rejection and childhood trauma.

Many try too hard to please others by agreeing with anything that is said or asked. They almost say "yes" before the question is asked, falling all over themselves to be approved and gain acceptance. Or, they may take exactly the opposite approach and not "knuckle under" to anyone or anything since to do so would be to demean themselves, and admit weakness and inferiority.

Those whom the person identifies with rejecting parents are singled out for more intense rejection. If a man is rejected by his mother he is very likely to do to his wife that which he didn't have the guts to do to his mother. The same is true when a woman has been rejected by her father.

In one instance where two such people were married the battle royale was decidedly in progress. When they saw the role that past rejection played in their dilemma the wife said "This is unfair. Why don't we get my father and his mother together and let *them* fight it out?" This couple as with others without number was caught in the crossfire generated by past rejection in totally unrelated families. The name of the game is "Rejection, pass it on!"

Another common behavior is that of clinging like a leech to the person who finally shows some love and acceptance. The reward is so great that he can't get enough and almost dogs the person's every step. The person has reached out to show love and any time spent with others, even consideration shown his own family, is considered a retraction of love or another rejection. Such jealousy is a common occurrence and the person who has newly found this panacea of acceptance will not readily let go of it for anything or anybody. When the other person attempts to set limits on the time involved he is made to feel guilty and this false guilt can spur him to spend an inordinate amount of time away from his own family. Thus, by loving an outsider in desperate need he has rejected his own.

The quiet desperation is fully exemplified in a family man in his 30's who had been rejected by all of the significant men in his life. His rejective attitudes had, in turn, carried over into his marriage with children being involved. A man in

53

need of a place to stay for a short while was invited with the wife's assent to spend the time in their home. With this man he finally found total acceptance and willingly traded his body for it, entering into a homosexual relationship which eventually necessitated rejecting his entire family.

## SUMMARY AND THE ANSWER, IN BRIEF

It should be self-evident that it is impossible to live in this world without some degree of rejection and rebuff. Alienation from the love of God is man's basic problem; reconciliation to God along with the restoration of His love and acceptance is the only complete answer.

Those who frequent the counselor's office have usually had a lion's share of rejection. The age at which it was experienced and the intensity of the rejection are the variables which determine the degree of devastation wrought in the life.

Acceptance on a supernatural level by God through the Lord Jesus Christ and discovering our identity in Him dissolves the rejection we have known on the natural level. Ephesians 1:6 states, "To the praise of the glory of his grace, wherein *he hath made us accepted in the beloved.*" In John 6:37 the same truth is restated, "All that the Father giveth me shall come to me; and *him that cometh to me I will in no wise cast out.*" In other words, "I *will* accept him."

Understanding our acceptance in Christ presupposes understanding our position in Christ. Identification with Christ and acceptance in Christ are like opposite sides of the same coin. If we know experientially we are accepted or acceptable in Christ, we will likewise have appropriated our identification with Him in His death, burial and resurrection. Conversely, if we know experientially that the corrupt sin nature has been dealt a death blow at the cross, we can accept our new risen self which is being conformed to His image (Romans 8:29). When we know that God accepts us we accept ourselves even if the whole world rejects us. When we know experientially our acceptance and glorious freedom in Christ (II Corinthians 5:17), we are set free from trying to please people. Then when others reject us (and they will), *they* have a problem! "And ye shall know the truth, and the truth shall make you free" (John 8:32).

### Acceptance

Oh, to know acceptance
 In a feeling sort of way;
To be known for what I am —
 Not what I do or say.
It's nice to be loved and wanted
 For the person I *seem* to be,
But my heart cries out to be loved
 For the person who is really *me*!

To be able to drop all the fronts
 And share with another my fears,
Would bring such relief to my soul,
 Though accompanied by many tears.
When I find this can be done
 Without the pain of rejection,
Then will my joy be complete
 And feelings toward self know correction.

The path to feeling acceptance of God.
 Is paved with acceptance on earth;
Being valued by others I love
 Enhances my own feeling of worth.
Oh, the release and freedom He gives
 As I behold His wonderful face —
As Jesus makes real my acceptance *in Him,*
 And I learn the true meaning of grace.

A pity it is that so late we find
His love need not be earned;
As we yield to Him all manner of strife
A precious truth has been learned.
Then, as we share with others who search
For love, acceptance, and rest;
They'll find in us the Savior's love.
And experience the end of their quest.

C. R. Solomon

## EXAMPLES OF REJECTION

Following are some examples of a person who has experienced rejection and the effects in the life and in interpersonal relationships.

### Example 1

A lady who had known rejection in her childhood was married and had children. True to form, she could not believe that her husband loved her. Since she was convinced that he rejected her, she openly rejected him. In fact, she tried to influence the children to hate and reject him, also. With no provocation from him except his presence, she would proceed to vent her hostility on him, verbally and physically. He would remain patient until she had spent her fury and then continue to relate to her as before. She was so petrified with fright she would have to have her children in bed with her for protection from demons, etc. She had been treated psychiatrically for some time. All of the foregoing behavior had its genesis in parental rejection.

As she was driving to church one day, she was singing "Calvary Love." When she came to the phrase, "I long to be worthy of Calvary love," the Holy Spirit checked her. She began to cry and exclaim, "I *am* accepted; I am *acceptable!*"

As the Holy Spirit revealed her acceptance, her hostility drained out and she knew the peace that passed all understanding. (Phillippians 4:7).

## EXAMPLE 2

Rejected and given away by her natural parents, a certain lady was further scarred by rejection in a foster home. The effects of this sent her into psychiatric treatment, both privately and institutionally. The lady with whom she lived while receiving counseling gave her a compliment about some work she had done. She became violently angry and proceeded to verbally castigate her friend. Neither of them could understand such illogical behavior.

The explanation was very simple. The commendation was totally at odds with her view of herself, which caused her to perceive it as ridicule. Such a person usually finds some way to prove that he should not have received a compliment, even for near-perfect work.

## EXAMPLE 3

A lady whose mother had deserted her as a small child and whose father had abused her could not believe that God loved her. Neither could she believe that the counselor was genuinely concerned for her. Although there was much progress early in the counseling relationship, it was perhaps two years before she could relax and rest in God's love. She is now being used of the Lord in ministering to others who have known rejection by loving them when they can not receive nor return the love.

## EXAMPLE 4

Jack and Jill are a classic case of mutual rejection. Jill's father had been unfaithful and left the home when she was a child. She experienced rejection by her father, resulting in a distrust of all men. Her mother did not want her to relate to her father even as an adult, which alienated the mother and daughter to some degree. She married Jack, an only child, who was told he was in the world because of the war. His father and grandfather were alcoholics so he was not only rejected but had no respect for men or the male sex. He and his wife shared this in common! He, therefore, rejected himself and his son (who had the misfortune of being male) while accepting his daughter. Their mutual rejection finally resulted in separation. She had accused him of being unfaithful from the inception of the marriage. As they saw their acceptance in Christ in less than a week of counseling, they were reunited. The transformation in their lives and marriage brought the brother-in-law in for counseling, and he trusted Christ in the first interview. Also, the father now accepts the son, and their relationship is radically changed.

## EXAMPLE 5

A lady who lost her father by death at age two could not relate to her stepfather or to other men except on a competitive basis. Even though her father had no choice in the rejection through his death, it had a profound influence on her life. She hardened herself into a sophisticate who needed no man and could compete with the best of them. Needless to say, she remained single. She set her goals in life and achieved them through intense self-effort but found a hollow victory.

# Rejection
# in the Church

A recurring theme which the Christian counselor hears repeated daily, if not hourly, is that the church is failing to meet the deepest needs of its individual members. In fact, this failure is the reason that he has clients. The psychologist and psychiatrist also exist for this reason. Many, if not most, of those frequenting the offices of the helping professions have first tried the church and have found that the liberal churches and some of the most fundamental churches fall short in meeting the mental and emotional needs of those in distress. A great number of those who are defeated and disturbed have in times past been very active in fundamental churches. Some have fallen into deep sin; others have put up a valiant fight against longstanding emotional and mental symptoms. After having exhausted all avenues of help in the church, which includes trying to grow through serving and working, the person is forced to go outside for help which usually means he is given some variety of the world's answer, such as psychotherapy.

So many times it is assumed that a person drops out of church because he has grown cold spiritually and has no desire for spiritual things. Although this may be his ultimate condition as he leaves the church, he may have been very zealous in his search for an answer and finally concludes that the church is impotent to meet his needs. Or, if he still has faith that the church, or God, has an answer which he cannot achieve, then he must be unworthy of God's love and care. This being the case, he may feel that God will meet the needs of others, but not his, and thus rejects him. And, he would logically turn from a supposedly "rejecting God" and His church to the appeal ot the world.

Where is the church failing? What is being done (or not being done) that turns persons off and alienates them from fellowship with God?

There are two main points of failure in the average church today: one is the lack of understanding of psychological or soulical needs, and the other is the absence of a concerted thrust to disciple those who are won to Christ. All of us have a driving passion to be understood and accepted even when we do not understand ourselves!

In church ministry our priorities can become so hopelessly entangled that we can't see the woods for the trees. When a person is won to Christ we emphasize service almost immediately. A new Christian very soon picks up the idea, by way of emphasis, that what he *does* is more important than what he *is*! If he ceases to be able to *do*, his feeling of worth to God, to others, and to himself deteriorates.

Most Christians have an identity problem and few understand the enormity of it. Still fewer have any idea as to the answer. From the time we are born we are brought up with the idea that what we are derives from what we produce; if we can't "produce" or "measure up" to the standards set by our parents, society, the church, or God we sense rejection by the foregoing and proceed to reject ourselves.

It is absolutely necessary to understand the rejection syndrome if one is going to appreciate what is happening in the church.

Since all of us in or out of the church have experienced various degrees of rejection, the effects of the rejection syndrome are of epidemic proportions. A person who has been rejected tends, in turn, to reject others making it only too obvious that the rejection syndrome must be operating within the church. None of the interrelationships is immune to its devastating effects, whether it be between those in the pews or between pastor and people.

What we are and the manner in which we see ourselves depends upon what or with whom we identify. If we identify with rejecting parents, we will ultimately experience self-rejection. This self-rejected parent has a faulty indentity which he passes along to his children, and the rejection syndrome thus repeats itself generation to generation.

The trauma of rejection is first experienced as a psychological problem in the soul or emotions since our identity has been established in relation to faulty and changeable humans. Though the rejection symptoms are psychological in origin, the answer lies in our identification with the immutable Lord Jesus Christ. We stop identifying with imperfect ones and identify, instead, with the Perfect One.

This identification is not an experiential reality with most Christians since the focus in the church is too often on what we *do* rather than what we *are* in Christ. As we grew up we got the idea that we were rejected if we failed to produce or "measure up." If the rejection were severe enough, the psychological symptoms might curtail our ability to produce to the point that we are unable to make the effort. This is frequently misinterpreted by church leadership as sloth-fulness or deliberate refusal to "get involved" in the work of the church. A person may sincerely desire to reach others for Christ through ministry in the church but is unable to resolve his own personal conflicts to make this a possibility.

Due to the lack of understanding of the rejection syndrome, much rejection takes place in the ministry of the church. The minister may unwittingly reject his people by admonishing them from the Word of God. On the surface this would appear to be paradoxical, but let's examine it a bit. Since the commands of Scripture to Christians are directed to Christ's divine nature (II Peter 1:4) in us, attempting to perform those commands after the flesh must end in frustration and defeat. If the minister exhorts his people to adhere to these commands without first leading them to an experiential understanding of their resources in Christ, he is rejecting his people. The individual's appropriation of *identification with Christ must precede spiritual service for Christ.* Service otherwise is simply the activity of self-effort.

Admonishing a Christian to perform beyond his spiritual maturity is rejection. Since the pastor is the spiritual leader or shepherd it is incumbent upon him to assist his people in assessing their spiritual growth and to avoid challenging them for spiritual service beyond their stage of growth. If a parent demanded that a three-week old baby go out and mow the lawn, all of the exhortation in the world would not enable the baby to perform the assigned task. All too frequently those in the church are equally ill prepared psychologically and/or spiritually to perform the scriptural injunctions for a life of holiness and service.

In turn, the laymen may reject those to whom they attempt to minister. Many soul-winning efforts are particularly susceptible to this malady. The recipient of a call in the home by those who sincerely desire to win him to Christ may sense a subtle rejection when the caller does not manifest an unselfish love. When the caller leads into some small talk, for example, about a family picture, and then jumps into challenging the person with the gospel, the one visited often feels manipulated rather than loved.

Conversely, when the caller manifests the love of Christ by showing consideration and a sincere desire to understand, love and accept the individual whether or not he is open to a gospel presentation, the door will always be open to a return call. It is an odd creature that will not respond to love when there are no strings attached.

Much church work is done out of a neurotic drive to gain acceptance and recognition on the part of the worker. Unknowingly, he is working to *get* rather than *give;* in reality he is exchanging services — doing for someone else to obtain that person's love, acceptance and gratitude. The worker also may really be seeking the acceptance of those who sent him out, (pastor, visitation chairman, etc.). Thus, he uses the person visited to satisfy his own unmet needs under the guise of "ministering the love of Christ" — which amounts to another subtle form of rejection.

A person comes to church to see how his spiritual and psychological needs can be met as well as to worship his Lord. If they are met he is then prepared to worship in spirit and in truth and go out to serve. However, when he earnestly strives to put into practice all he has been taught and fails to establish a meaningful relationship, he senses rejection. Many such people generalize from the people of the church to God and feel that God has rejected them, too. The obvious result is to respond in kind by saying in essence: "You've rejected me, so I will reject you." The result is that another spiritual unfortunate is added to the "church dropout culture."

The sojourn in and exodus from the church based upon a rejection experience is a serious matter affecting many people. Individuals are part of families; families have associates or groups of friends (sometimes known as cliques). These individuals and groups comprise the local church, and local churches band together in a denomination or association. The rejection syndrome knows no bounds and runs the gamut from the individual to the denominational structure. Proper understanding of the effect on the whole must begin with an understanding of the constituent persons.

## THE CHURCH DROPOUT CULTURE

To illustrate some of the steps in the dropout process, let's take a look at a composite picture of experiences that many have had. This trend has been extracted from those seen in the counseling office over a period of years. For ease of expression the male example is used; however, the pattern could as easily be applied to the female.

Let's pick up the story where a man has become aware of a need in his life and realizes through the ministry of the Holy Spirit that he is lost. His life of sin may have evolved into a series of problems involving attitudes, motivation, emotional disturbances, behavior, etc. In God's timing he is presented with the gospel plan of salvation from the Word of God. He learns that he is a sinner and that the Lord Jesus Christ died for his sins, was buried and rose again according to the Scriptures (I Corinthians 15:3). Since he was convicted of sin, he receives Christ as Savior and is born again or regenerated.

Immediately upon his new birth he is dealt with from the Word regarding assurance of his salvation. Although, too frequently he is asked the inane question as soon as he says "Amen": "How do you *feel*?" This may seem very innocent, but he gets the message that he should feel something if he is born again. This simple question can counteract all the teaching given to him about his assurance being based on the Word of God. First, he gets the idea that he isn't saved unless he felt something; and then, later on, he begins to doubt his salvation if he ceases to *feel* saved. Through this simple error, many are locked into a lifetime of feeling unsaved.

This lack of assurance of salvation bears some explanation.

It is possible for a person to go for years *feeling* unsaved and never *doubt* his salvation. Feeling unsaved is a product of the emotions whereas doubting one's salvation is a mental or intellectual problem. Too frequently, the counselor working with a person who feels unsaved vainly tries to prove to him from the Word that he is saved. The person who has no reservations about the Scriptures and knows that he accepted Christ at a point in the past, concludes intellectually that he is saved yet *feels* that he isn't. When he is told that he is calling God a liar if he doesn't believe what the Word says, he has more guilt heaped upon the "unsaved feeling" in his emotions which compounds his problem. Thus locked into wrong emotions, the person is launched into his career of church membership.

He is properly dealt with about the importance of study in the Word, fellowship with other believers and is taken into the church with the good wishes of all concerned.

Discipleship may now take the form of one-way communication — pulpit to pew or teacher to student — where information about the Word is thrown "at" him. Little or no one-on-one personal discipleship training is involved. A form of rejection by being "one of the crowd" occurs since the personal attention so much desired is not available.

Since he is "new blood" and there is much work to be done, he is challenged to go to work immediately even though he is merely a babe in Christ. However, he is convinced that it is God's honest due that he work for Him in return for what God has done for him. The coercion from the church leadership may take the form of "God had done so much for you, can't you do this little bit for him?" Many times he is given more than one job since he wants to "get into the harness" and very rapidly finds himself so busy *for* God that he has little time left to spend *with* God. Since there is a flurry of activity there is also some productivity as God honors His Word.

After a period of months or years this initial zeal wanes and a person no longer gets the emotional kicks from all the work he is doing. Since his feelings are in need of "pumping up," he "goes forward" to rededicate his life to Christ. He then redoubles *his* effort to do God's work. This makes him feel better for a while since he has "humbled" himself at the altar and has resolved to do more *for* the Lord. As he fails in his resolve he begins to feel more guilty and repeats the process. One man put it this way: "I tripped to the altar so many times that my rededicator wore out."

As time passes he begins to reach the point of diminishing returns for time and effort spent. His output is sagging and the challenges from the pulpit begin to cause increased guilt since he isn't "measuring up." The guilt adds to his already pressing emotional problems. Since he has tried everything he knows to be able to "produce" and is still unable to find fulfillment, the only way he sees to reduce the guilt is to avoid the challenge. He begins to withdraw from responsibility so he cannot be taken to task for failure to be faithful in his commitments. When partial withdrawal is challenged by church leadership to the point where he becomes uncomfortable, he withdraws completely by dropping out of church or backsliding.

At this point his wife enters the scene and coerces the pastor into dealing with the dropout at home. In many instances the pastor's visit creates a sense of further rejection and increased guilt. Instead of being understood and having his resources in Christ explained to him, the backslider feels "put down" and loses face with his family; thus, the rejection syndrome is compounded.

Appropriately, bitterness builds within him because of the failure of the church to meet his needs. Unfortunately, he generalizes this to Christ and his bitterness doesn't stop with the church. Eventually, the bitterness and resentment along with the methods he uses to ease the pain and frustration (such as alcohol or some other escape effort) cause his wife and the church to conclude that he is a "professor" but not a "possessor."

Now he is left with the conclusion that he is not a Christian and has no way for God to meet his needs. Since he is accorded very little empathy, understanding and love, he concludes that all Christians are hypocrites and berates his wife about going to church. His wife staunchly defends her Christianity while defying the headship of her husband in many areas. Though the wife is not in submission to her husband and is locked into her self-righteousness, the church defends her position and prays for her husband. Eventually, she concludes that it is easier to switch than fight and drops out of church as a martyr.

Since the wife does not submit to her husband's authority and he isn't in submission to God's authority the children are taught by example not to respect authority. Since the home is the place they should learn obedience, they may soon be in defiance of school and/or civil authority and ultimately reject the authority of God.

Thus, the family is lost to the church, and the husband receives the blame while the church maintains its standards and continues to lay the burden on the believer to do in his own strength what only Christ can do in and through him. Since this process is on-going in several families at the same time, the factions of a dissident group band together and begin to vent their hostility on the leadership and the pastor. Since the dissident group feels its cause is right there is some satisfaction gained by fighting and trying to promote that cause.

The church misses the whole point of what is going on and defends its position while placing the blame on the dissident group. The symptoms are blown out of proportion due to the emotional fervor of those seeking relief and not having their resources in Christ explained to them. The situation is frequently "resolved" by a church split.

Both groups contend they have a righteous cause and a new church is started by the dissenting faction. The new church is too busy pulling together toward the common cause of building and enjoying growth to see that the seeds for dissension and dropout are present. Many such churches contend that God was in the split even though the carnality in the break-up is usually evident to the most casual observer. Indeed, the world has every reason to say, "See how they hate one another!" Once the new church stabilizes, the absolute necessity of pulling together is past and the slack allows the above process to be inevitably set in motion all over again.

Meanwhile, back at the old church the pastor resolves his guilt and failure symptoms by affirming to himself and his reduced congregation that those who left could not endure strong preaching of the gospel (the substitutionary aspects of the cross). He continues to feed his people a liquid diet of milk while continuing to "tongue lash" them to produce more work. Altar calls are sometimes so broad that anyone who resists would, in effect, be saying he is perfect; so great numbers line the altar which gives the pastor a vote of confidence. The reduced numbers in the church and the urgency of the situation causes the church to regroup and pull together to rebuild, at least for a short time.

After repeating this process one or more times, the pastor moves to a new field. The "honeymoon" is soon over and the above process takes place at the new field. Eventually, the pastor is forced to realize that all of the responsibility cannot be borne by the various congregations. There must be something he is or isn't doing! However, just as with the lay person, he has no one in whom to confide who can show him how his personal and professional needs can be met. This may be even more true since "Pastor to flock" pride often precludes true sharing. As he begins to have some emotional problems it is not only a personal catastrophe, it is also a professional hazard! The needs of the people and pastor alike are not being met (and as a minister he should have the answer), so he has no choice but to *drop out.*

Since he wants to save face he may accept a teaching or administrative position or go to the mission field to remain in full-time work. If he teaches, he will reproduce himself; if he goes to the mission field, "personality conflicts" are likely to develop; and the administrative position is unlikely to give him the fulfillment he knew as a pastor. If he does not avail himself of one of the above escapes or copouts, his emotional problems may become so severe that he will be asked to leave the pastorate. As he comes to the end of his resources, he is forced to resign and seek employment for which he is not trained such as insurance sales, etc.

To take the dropout scene just one step further, with the above process on-going in several churches simultaneously, it is only logical that the dissenting churches should unite in a common cause of defending some aspect of the faith or denominational practice and the denomination or association begins to polarize around some issue or institution. As the emotions become more heated the issues become more blurred. The stage is now set for the dropout of a segment of the association, denomination, convention, etc., and the formation of a conservative, right or pure group established to carry on the banner for Christ, thus launching The Dropout Culture *en masse.*

Church history is replete with splits and schisms in churches, church bodies, and seminaries — all of which do great damage to those within the church. This also compounds the dismay of those outside the organized church and outside of Christ.

All of this is in spite of the fact that our Savior prayed:
"That they all may be one; as thou, Father, art in me, and I in Thee, that they also may be one in us: *that the world may believe that thou hast sent me*" (John 17:21).

69

# The Message
# of the Church

### INSTRUCTION IN RECONCILIATION

Why have some churches failed to know the empowering of the Holy Spirit for service and for loving one another? And why are divisions often more prevalent than the unity of the Spirit? What is missing in churches where many are saved but so few discipled? Let's look at an overview of what is currently being taught in fundamental churches. Some solid fundamental churches fall down on points within this framework, but the majority are faithful in emphasizing the points illustrated.

The following diagram serves to illustrate in somewhat of a sequential manner the concepts taught a new believer. Unfortunately, few Christians go beyond that presented in this diagram.

The diagram gives some indication of the manner in which a person progresses, and those who successfully negotiate this course and avoid the widely known taboos (or no-no's) are commonly accepted as "mature" Christians. Each point will only be covered briefly since volumes have been written on each of the above points discussed.

The first, conviction of sin, is common to all who subsequently believe on the name of the Lord Jesus Christ and are born again. The Word teaches that one cannot come to the Lord Jesus unless the Holy Spirit draws him. Thus, he recognizes that he is a sinner, believing that the Lord Jesus Christ died for him, was buried and rose again. Upon believing the gospel, he prays some form of the sinner's prayer and is born again or saved (2).

Although the Word teaches that we should accept Jesus Christ as Savior and Lord, many do not understand what it means to yield the total control of their lives at the time of the new birth. Therefore, it is necessary that the Lordship commitment (3) be made at some subsequent time. This is a volitional choice, an act of the will according to Romans 12:1. This constitutes an abandonment to God of all rights to one's self which few Christians ever do. Since this is the case, Romans 12:2 — being transformed by the renewing of the mind — is never a reality for most Christians.

Next, (4), the new believer is shown the importance of knowing that his assurance is to be based on the Word of God — not on fluctuating feelings. Feelings may be at variance with fact. Even though well-adjusted, feelings are fleeting at best and not to be trusted. The danger involved in asking a person how he feels was presented in the previous chapter. God's Word is unchanging, and our assurance will be secure as long as we see and accept with our wills, by an act of faith, our position in Christ as it is delineated in Scripture.

Even though controversial in vast segments of Christianity, the security (5) of the believer is held to be vital to healthy spiritual growth. Unless a person can rest in his secure position in Christ, he feels compelled to work to maintain his salvation. He may hold that salvation is by faith alone in what Christ has done, but he resorts to faith plus works in order to remain saved. The believer's security is to be based

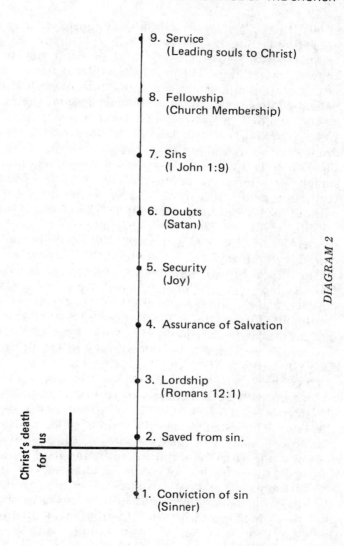

THE BLOOD

Christ's death for us

DIAGRAM 2

9. Service
   (Leading souls to Christ)

8. Fellowship
   (Church Membership)

7. Sins
   (I John 1:9)

6. Doubts
   (Satan)

5. Security
   (Joy)

4. Assurance of Salvation

3. Lordship
   (Romans 12:1)

2. Saved from sin.

1. Conviction of sin
   (Sinner)

solidly on the Word just as in his assurance. He may lose his joy without losing his salvation (Psalm 51:12).

Most personal workers would then point out to a new convert that Satan will try to get him to doubt (6) his salvation. It is important for the new believer to know that Satan operates in this manner now just as with Adam and Eve when he tried to cast doubt on the veracity of God's Word. Next (7) new believers are shown the necessity of dealing with sins and are told that we have an advocate with the Father (I John 2:1) if we should sin. First John 1:9 is sometimes referred to as the Christian's bar of soap. This is very appropriate since it deals with the result of defilement without (sins) but does not get to the source within (the self-life or flesh). This being the case, the Christians finds himself in a vicious cycle of confession, reminiscent of Paul's experience in Romans 7.

The fellowship of believers (8), usually involving church membership, baptism, etc., is most important for the new believer and is imperative if he is to continue to grow spiritually. First John 1:3 ties together our fellowship with one another and our fellowship with the Lord Jesus Christ: ". . . that ye also may have fellowship with us: and truly our fellowship is with the Father, and with his Son Jesus Christ."

Once he is grounded in the basics and has a place of fellowship with other believers, it is properly pointed out to the new believer (9) that he is to be involved in service for the Lord. This usually takes the form of holding office in the church or teaching or winning souls to Christ. Even though soul winning is frequently held to be the mark of a mature Christian, such efforts may be carried out after the flesh.

The foregoing may be subsumed under the heading of The Blood since the blood primarily deals with sins as opposed to the cross which deals with sin — that is, the source of sins or the power of sin. (See Chapter 1 and 2 of The Normal Christian Life by Watchman Nee).

It is not intended that any of the above point be omitted or de-emphasized but that the following receive equal emphasis with the new Christian.

## Instruction in Spiritual Maturity

Most of the above points are cardinal in the teaching of a fundamental church and rightfully so; yet the dropout system described above is perpetuated in spite of such sound scriptural teaching. What is missing? How are the seeds of dissension built into a doctrinally right system of teaching? It seems that most Christians who go on to maturity have to learn lessons (1) to (9) over again at a deeper level.

It is not to be inferred that a "two step" or "second blessing" approach is herein advocated. This is merely a description of "what is." It is the position of the author that the tenets of both diagrams 2 and 3 should be taught simultaneously to new believers.

Let's reiterate the above points and see some deeper meanings not learned nor appropriated by many Christians and, therefore, not clearly taught in many churches of any denomination or persuasion.

Just as an unbeliever must see himself as a sinner by revelation of the Holy Spirit, so must a believer see the despicable nature of the flesh or self. The unbeliever is convicted of sin; the believer must be convicted of self (1) if he is to see the need for it to be dealt with by the cross. As long as he thinks there is something good in the flesh with which he can successfully serve the Lord, he is deceived and his growth will be stunted. He may be a successful soul winner, evangelist, or pastor and not recognize the place that self-effort or the flesh takes in his ministry. Therefore, the Holy Spirit must show him through the Word and/or cause him to fail in some manner to force him to see the deceitfulness of his flesh or self-life. Once the true picture of the repulsive self-life is clearly seen, he will be ready and

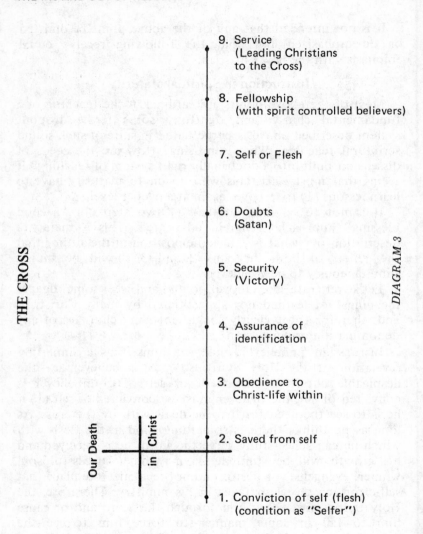

*DIAGRAM 3*

THE CROSS

Our Death / in Christ

9. Service
(Leading Christians
to the Cross)

8. Fellowship
(with spirit controlled believers)

7. Self or Flesh

6. Doubts
(Satan)

5. Security
(Victory)

4. Assurance of
identification

3. Obedience to
Christ-life within

2. Saved from self

1. Conviction of self (flesh)
(condition as "Selfer")

thankful to appropriate by faith the victory that is rightfully his through his (2) crucifixion, burial, and resurrection with Christ (Romans 6:4-6).

Previously he saw he was saved or reconciled to God by the death of His Son (Romans 5:10a); now he sees that he was also saved from himself! According to Romans 5:10b, he is saved from himself (delivered from the dominion of sin) by the life of Christ within. Even though co-crucifixion was a reality when he was born again as far as God was concerned, his identification with Christ in death, burial, resurrection and ascension was not explained to him nor appropriated by him at the time of salvation. Once a person is convicted of his condition as a *selfer* and sees the scriptural remedy for that condition, he is ready to pray a selfer's prayer and claim by faith his death, burial, resurrection, ascension, and seating with Christ. Just as in accepting Christ as Savior there is to be no dependence on feelings for confirmation that God has done a work in the human spirit, there is to be no emphasis on feelings in appropriating Christ as our life.

Obedience (3) to the Christ-life within corresponds to the Lordship commitment and is equally important. However, it requires more spiritual discernment to yield to the Christ-life than to attempt to obey in his own strength the clear injunctions of the Word as interpreted by pastor, teacher or himself. It appears more logical to the self-life that it is easier to try to keep rules with your own fleshly strength than to admit you can't and let Christ be your life instead.

Assurance (4) that the Christ-life has been appropriated (identification) based on the Word (Romans 6:6,11,13) is equally as important as assurance of salvation. Although there is generally a new freedom from the problem of the flesh as the Christ-life is appropriated, assurance is not based on the life changes but on the unchanging truth of God. When our assurance is based on the Word, we can never be shaken when we have temporary "down times."

Security (5) in our identification with Christ is also parallel to our security in salvation. Though we may feel defeated or doubt our position in Christ, it is as secure as the Lord Jesus' position at the right hand of God because we are in Him there! Though our victory is assured as we rest in the Victor, the battles may be more fierce than those encountered in the Wilderness. We have entered the Promised Land but we must maintain a faith position that all our enemies are vanquished! We may lose our *victory* temporarily but not our position or Possession.

Since we are accustomed to defeat and feel this must continue to be our lot, Satan would again tempt us to turn from our sure promises and look within and be defeated (6). As at all other stages of our growth, Satan's prime tactic is to undermine the Word of God. Since faith is the victory and the Word is the basis for our faith, it is of utmost importance that we treat as suspect any inward or outward condition which will lead us to turn from reliance upon God's Word.

As in previous stages of growth we must continue to confess or acknowledge our sins (I John 1:9). But it is of great importance that we go beyond confession of a sin and continuously allow God to deal with the self-life or the flesh (7). Although "our old man" died with Christ once for all (Romans 6:6,10,11), there must be the daily (Luke 9:23) and continuous (II Corinthians 4:11) reckoning upon or counting upon that death to sin that we might maintain victory over the flesh. As we choose against ourselves and reckon upon the Christ-life within, He can keep us in unbroken victory as the "law of the Spirit of life in Christ Jesus" frees us from "the law of sin and death" (Romans 8:2).

Fellowship (8) with other believers never loses its importance at any stage of growth. Particularly, in spiritual warfare we must have other believers who can pray for us at a time when our prayer may seem to be all but ineffective.

Since there are so few believers who have appropriated the abundant or abiding life, the necessary fellowship is not so readily available as it is for the new believer.

Service (9) takes on a new character when the dimension of discipleship is added. Luke 14:27 states that we are not disciples unless we have taken up the cross.

Previously, the goal of service was to win others to Christ; and this goal remains an imperative. Now the goal is to lead these and those already Christians to the cross that they might be freed from the bondage of the self-life. As this emancipation is realized, these Christians will have victory to share with others so that they may begin to fulfill the unique ministry to which they are called, either in a vocational capacity or along with their occupation or profession.

## SUMMARY

As the reader has probably already noted, there is much more emphasis placed on evangelism than on discipleship by the great preponderance of churches. Since this is the case, many believers live their entire lives without even knowing that appropriation of the victorious life is a live option. Therefore, the self-life or flesh is in the ascendancy in the majority of Christians. This being the case, it is only too natural that the self-lives should clash and cause the drop-out activity described in the previous chapter.

If we as Christians are going to provide the answer that only we can give to a world that is rapidly headed for disaster, it is absolutely necessary that we appropriate Christ as *our* life so that the world may see Him in His fullness, unity and power — not our self-life with its confusion, disharmony and weakness of worldly methods, to say nothing of the more corrupt works of the flesh.

The prime goal is not to keep our members from dropping out and our churches from splitting but to offer the world a united front by maintaining "the unity of the Spirit in the bond of peace" (Ephesians 4:3). If we are to be able to continue winning souls to Christ, it is now absolutely necessary that we teach our believers so that the miraculous in lives will become common place rather than exceptional. When the world begins to see the power of the cross, replacing the weakness of the flesh, then the Lord Jesus Christ will be lifted up and men will be drawn to Him, whom to know is life eternal.

When God's people are truly empowered by His Spirit to reach the world for which He sent His only Son to die, then, and only then, can we say that it is ". . . Not by might, nor by power, but by my spirit, saith the Lord of hosts" (Zechariah 4:6).

# Part 2.

# THE WAY OUT
## OR
# THE CROSS

# PREFACE TO PART TWO

The way out of a discouraged, defeated, and/or psychologically disturbed life is the way of the cross. The manner in which the cross is appropriated experientially in the life is carefully spelled out in my book, "Handbook To Happiness". This is an addendum which will help the reader to understand more of the dynamics of Spirituotherapy and the manner in which insights from the scriptures can be shared in a counseling setting or by the layman.

In addition to my personal testimony, insights and observations gathered over the last few years have been included.

## IMPORTANT NOTE

Some of the definitions assigned in Part Two, especially in Chapter 6, are a departure from the commonly accepted theological terminology. This has been done in an attempt to combine the terminology of the psychologist and the theologian into functional relationships. This effects an integration of the two disciplines which is intended to give pre-eminence to the Lord Jesus Christ, the infallibility and immutability of the Word of God, and to hold out the scriptural answer to man's problems in living as well as in dying.

While the biblical model of man which is sufficient to explain the totality of human behavior is implicit in the diagrams, terminology and text which follow, development of a definitive model which can be published is still under way at Grace Fellowship International (GFI). In like manner the counseling theory, from constructs to implementation, is in the developmental stages and its completion is sorely needed, not only for use at GFI, but also to explain implications and applications for both disciplines.

The King James Version has been utilized as a common denominator, but the reader should take special note of differing definitions and study carefully the usage in text and diagram before assuming understanding or reacting on the basis of past knowledge or prejudice.

This presentation is not intended to be the last word, but rather an initial foray into the no-man's land which has traditionally separated the disciplines of psychology and theology. Information which will serve the purpose of clarifying or correcting the material presented will be gratefully received and perused for integration into subsequent study, research, and publication.

# A Life In Turmoil

The author has found it helpful in gaining rapport with an individual and with groups, to share his life or portions of it under the leading of the Holy Spirit. When a person realizes that Spirituotherapy was not learned in the academic setting but hammered out in a life and later crystallized into a counseling process, he may conclude that it could work for him as well. And it can! Accordingly, I would like to share a first-person testimony so that some may identify with this life and then go on to identify with the One who is *the* Life — the Lord Jesus Christ.

## Early Years

I was born in rural East Tennessee in 1930 at the very beginning of the depression. My father was a sharecropper on the farm of his widowed mother. My mother was in ill health at the time of my birth and was not really well for the first two years of my life. I was the second of four children, having three sisters. My paternal grandmother was very protective of her children, and my father was affected by this characteristic. He was also the second child and felt it necessary to compete with his older brother for his father's acceptance and never quite made it. His feelings of inferiority and insecurity played a definite role in the development of these same attitudes within myself.

Until I was about six we lived in a farmhouse which had no insulation, no underpinning, no heating stove (an ineffective fireplace supplied some heat), no electricity, no running water, and insufficient bedroom space for three children. We then moved to another community where the living conditions were about the same except for the fact that we were buying the house and a small acreage. My father began in carpentry and went on to be highly respected in heavy construction.

My parents were Christians who loved me very much and trained me to the best of their ability in the things of the Lord. I know they have prayed for me all during the years. My mother improved in health but worked much too hard due to the lack of modern conveniences.

I did very well in school but was totally crushed if I had to spend any amount of time in learning such things as multiplication tables; I felt I should know them immediately. My first memory of feeling inferior in school work was upon my promotion to sixth grade; this meant going upstairs and I felt it would be too difficult for me. However, I reasoned that I could accomplish nothing by repeating fifth grade and so I pushed myself to do something which I felt I couldn't do. This was to become a pattern of life.

The junior high years were rather uneventful. I was of slight build which added to my inferiority feelings, especially in confrontation situations or in body contact sports. As I went into high school (ninth grade) at the age of thirteen, my slight stature continued to be a sore point. Also, I didn't like my facial features; in short, I didn't like me! I felt everyone in my class knew more than I did and yet I expected to receive better marks than they, and I usually did. I could never excel at sports and my high marks were a source of rejection rather than acceptance on the part of my peers. It never occurred to me that any of my teachers might be interested in me as a person. I only saw them as people who could be obstacles if I let them know too much about myself. Although most of them were friendly and seemed to like me, I would never dare let down the front and reveal my inner fears to them. There were some happy times during high school, but I was greatly relieved when I was able to get beyond it and attempt to start a new life.

To go back and pick up my spiritual history, I had attended several "revival" meetings in which I saw the need for a Savior. On about three occasions I had "gone forward" and several persons would kneel around me and talk to the Lord but none had the good sense to talk with me. Therefore, I went away each time without coming to know the Lord Jesus Christ. At about age seventeen, I determined one night to pray in my bed until I knew that the Lord had saved me. There was no emotional experience but the quiet calm peace that I was His became an established fact. However, having had no one to lead me *to* Christ, I also had no one to lead me *in* Christ.

Shortly afterward, I was faced with the decision about college. The"moving upstairs"syndrome again plagued me. I felt I was too stupid to train for a profession such as law or the ministry since stage fright made it impossible for me to speak publicly. Even so, the thought of the ministry did go through my mind; but I promptly dismissed it as ridiculous. At about age seven my minister, Mr. Willis Johnson, placed his hand on my head on leaving the church one day and told my parents that I would make a good minister. That meant little at the time, but I never forgot it.

I felt that I had to try college and since I had fairly high marks in mathematics I decided to study engineering. I enrolled in East Tennessee State University in a pre-engineering course. I studied very hard because I was afraid I would flunk out and, true to form, came up with straight A's the first quarter. I concluded the work was not very difficult if I could do it, so the straight A's did little to bolster my self-confidence.

Beginning college was a good experience in some ways. The professors called me by my first name whereas I had grown up using my second. In a sense I felt I was a new person, but at the same time I realized I was the same inferior-feeling person despite the new name. However, I was able to start over without my new friends knowing all of my faults. There were many happy times as I learned to live away from home and involved myself in new activities. I visited church occasionally but had no fellowship and no direct challenge toward spiritual growth during these four years of college. I met my wife, Sue, during the second year and we dated regularly through my junior year. By this time I had decided that I had neither the intelligence nor the money to switch to an engineering school. Accordingly, I majored in mathematics and received a teaching certificate.

I had informed my fiancée about my inferiority feelings, but she refused to believe me because of the front I presented. Despite the feelings of inferiority and insecurity, we proceeded to get married between my junior and senior years with neither of us employed. A month later she got a teaching job and I commuted 100 miles daily to complete my senior year. As graduation approached I was faced with the possibility of military duty in Korea or securing employment in essential industry. I elected to apply to Glenn L. Martin Co. in Baltimore, Maryland and was hired by mail as an engineering draftsman. But I was neither an engineer nor a draftsman! I had had a couple of engineering drawing courses, so I proceeded to fight the "moving upstairs" syndrome again.

Although I felt I could not handle the work, two years and one son later, I had six men working for me. This was to begin a period of about five years during which I had the supervisory responsibility for up to twenty-five men. Some of the men were twice my age, and many had more engineering education and experience than I. I found myself supervising men who performed tasks I had never done. This, along with sin in my life, as well as increased family pressures, began to take their toll.

The day my first daughter was born, I was assigned the responsibility of supervising the installation design of the fuel system of a medium jet. As the job went on I began to have a voracious appetite and gained 25 pounds in six months. Anxiety increased to the point that I was put on tranquilizers and subsequently found I was feeding a duodenal ulcer. At about the time our second daughter was born, I was taking 400 mg of Thorazine per day while driving my car and continuing with my work. When I received the call that my wife was having our baby, I thought they said it was my mother. I started to place a long-distance call and checked myself saying, "That's impossible! My mother couldn't be having a baby." So I proceeded to go back to work. A little later the truth broke through, and I raced for the hospital to find my daughter was twenty minutes old.

My mental and emotional state drove me to try many things to find help. Since I was already a Christian and that didn't help, I looked elsewhere. Everything I did was misinterpreted by my wife as rejection of her and our children which made matters worse rather than better. Although I knew she loved me, there would be times at work that I felt I would lose my mind in my longing just to hear her say, "I love you." The intensity of my anxiety and being out of touch with reality at times began to cause her problems as well.

By January 1957, I decided to submit totally my life to the Lord Jesus Christ as the only possible means of maintaining my sanity and, probably, my marriage. Again in my bedroom I yielded my life to Him without reservation. Of course, no one (including my wife) knew this so I had no guidance as to how to proceed.

I decided to start studying the Bible so I got up early each morning and read in Genesis. There are better places to study for spiritual growth, but this was better than nothing. I became active in a liberal church and tried to serve the Lord. My mental and emotional adjustment improved to some extent but my wife saw my church involvement as another copout so it was less than satisfying. About two years later, after we had bought a small home, I learned that our company was interviewing for positions in Denver. I decided privately that an offer of $50 per month increase would be an indication we should move to Denver. The offer was exactly $50, so I went home and announced we were moving! Within three weeks our house was sold (without a realtor), and we were on our way.

The Lord led us to a Bible-believing church where we are still members. I began to memorize Scripture using the Navigator system and did much compulsive work in the church. I still could not stand myself enough to be quiet at home. I taught Sunday school, went calling, became a deacon and did many other things which caused me to neglect my family.

On March 27, 1964 (my youngest daughter's birthday), I attended a college-age retreat at The Navigators international headquarters in Colorado Springs. During a lecture by Mr. Lorne Sanny, the Holy Spirit seemed to impress some Scripture passages upon me from Isaiah 60. These are Isaiah 60:1: "Arise, shine; for thy light is come, and the glory of the Lord is risen upon thee"; Isaiah 60:15: "Whereas thou was forsaken and hated, *so that no man went through thee, I* will make thee an eternal excellency, a joy of many generations"; Isaiah 60:22: "A little one shall become a thousand, and a small one a strong nation: I the Lord will hasten it in his time."

During a time apart from the group I was studying the Word and came across Psalm 37:3-5: "Trust in the Lord, and do good; so shalt thou dwell in the land, and verily thou shalt be fed. Delight thyself also in the Lord; and he shall give thee the desires of thine heart. Commit thy way unto the Lord; trust also in him; and *he shall bring it to pass.*" As I read this passage I broke into tears; the Holy Spirit witnessed that this was a direct promise to me—the first such promise in my life— at age thirty-four. I hadn't the slightest notion as to what the promise was to entail but I knew that God had promised to "bring it to pass," whatever it was. But then I began to wonder — "Who do you think you are that God could use you? If He were going to do so He would have started before now. Your life is half over; it's too late to get into something different." These and a myriad of other thoughts vied for my attention. I alternated between believing that God had spoken and being totally incredulous that such a thing could be.

Needless to say, I didn't share this with Sue since I thought she would feel, as I did most of the time, that this was just another of my many tangents. She could not accept the fact of my feelings of inferiority and insecurity even though we had now been married about fourteen years. Therefore, the more I hurt, the more she hurt but we bore our hurt in silence. There were attempts on both parts to reach across the chasm without success. We shared the same home and the children, some good and bad times; but in the innermost recesses of our hearts, we walked alone.

## ALONE TOGETHER

We walked alone together,
  My precious wife and I,
Nor learned to share our burdens,
  But only how to sigh.

Our hearts being knit in love
  Yearned for sweet communion;
But it seemed that such a joy
  Could not grace our union.

The burdens that we carried
  Seemed oft too much to bear,
But no matter how we tried
  We could not the trials share.

The burdens served God's purpose (Ps. 119:71)
  To drive us to our knees;
As we fellowshipped with Christ (Phil.3:10)
  He taught us by degrees. (Isa.28:9,10)

As His purpose for our lives (Rom. 8:29)
  Began to come to pass, (Ps. 37:5)
We saw that inner conflict (Phil. 1:29,30)
  Had been our training class. (Heb. 12:11)

The comfort that He gave us
  Was ours to keep in store;
Those who likewise walk alone (Ps. 142:4)
  Find comfort at our door. (2 Cor. 1:3,4)

We praise our precious Saviour
  In Him our life is found; (Phil. 1:21)
Though we are ever failing
  In Him doth grace abound. (2 Cor. 9:8)

94

The fears that came between us
  Were like a mighty tower;
But Jesus made them tumble
  By His transforming power. (Rom. 12:2)

And now we walk together
  In growing harmony;
Our burdens become lighter
  When borne by me and thee. (Gal. 6:2)

As we share from heart to heart
  Our love is fused with peace;
As the years slip swiftly by
  Our joy but knows increase.

C. R. Solomon

Though at times I was relatively certain I had a promise from the Lord, depression and anxiety remained a way of life. My ulcer had been healed by the Lord in 1960 but other psychosomatic ailments continued to persist. As there was no tangible reason to believe that the Lord was to intervene in the affairs of my life, the financial responsibilities of my family loomed larger and larger. I began to worry about being laid off from my position and thought it would be better if we sold our home. This appeared logical to me at the time. We had one or two persons look at the house but we had no offers so the sign came down after a period of time.

As I read the Word and spent time in prayer, I searched for confirmation of God's promise. At times I would weep on the way home from work and silently weep in my pillow at night. I worried because I couldn't meet the needs of my wife and children; I worried because I couldn't meet my *own* needs. I knew that the anxiety which racked my body was taking its toll. I had no one who could understand the

95

depth of the turmoil I endured, and most of the time I didn't believe God understood or cared.

In my agony of soul I searched the Bible for additional light on what God wanted me *to do,* little realizing that He was first interested in what He wanted me *to be.* Nevertheless, He was faithful to give me something to hold on to while He continued His processing. It was destined to be nineteen more painful months before release from bondage was to come. The following are some of the words from the Lord which I grasped for varying lengths of time as the tunnel became blacker and longer.

April, '64

Isaiah 43:18,19: "Remember ye not the former things, neither consider the things of old. Behold, I will do a new thing; now it shall spring forth; shall ye not know it? I will even make a way in the wilderness, and rivers in the desert."

Isaiah 46:11b: ". . . yea, I have spoken it, I will also bring it to pass; I have purposed it, I will also do it."

Isaiah 50:7: "For the Lord God will help me; therefore shall I not be confounded; therefore have I set my face like a flint, and I know that I shall not be ashamed."

May, '64

Habbakkuk 2:3: *"For the vision is yet for an appointed time, but at the end it shall speak, and not lie; though it tarry, wait for it; because it will surely come, it will not tarry."*

Colossians 4:17: "Take heed to the ministry which thou has received in the Lord, that thou fulfil it."

June, '64

Hebrews 4:9,10: "There remaineth therefore a rest to the people of God. For he that is entered into his rest, he also hath ceased from his own works, as God did from his."

July, '64

I Samuel 12:16: "Now therefore stand and see this great

thing, which the Lord will do before your eyes."

September, '64

Hebrews 12:3: "For consider him . . . lest ye be wearied and faint in your minds."

November, '64

I Samuel 10:6: "And the Spirit of the Lord will come upon thee, and thou shalt prophecy with them, and shalt be turned into another man."

In November, 1964, my psychosomatic symptoms were diagnosed by a neurologist as multiple sclerosis but a spinal tap during hospitalization failed to support his diagnosis. I was privately disappointed that it was not cancer so I could get an honorable discharge from life. Many times prior to this I had envied senior citizens who had "made it through" and didn't have to fight it much longer.

November, '64

Isaiah 40:26: (In the hospital) "Lift up your eyes on high, and behold who hath created these things, that bringeth out their host by number: he calleth them all by names by the greatness of his might, for that he is strong in power; not one faileth."

Isaiah 42:16: (After the hospital) "And I will bring the blind by a way that they knew not; I will lead them in paths that they have not known: I will make darkness light before them and crooked things straight. These things will I do unto them and not forsake them."

March, '65

Isaiah 54:4: "Fear not, for thou shalt not be ashamed: neither be thou confounded; for thou shalt not be put to shame."

I desperately needed this last promise because my depression was deepening and, to make matters worse, I was elected chairman of the board of deacons in my church. At my place of employment, personnel continued to be laid off on a sporadic basis and my emotional instability did little to commend me for continued employment. If I were laid off in this condition, what could I possibly do? The Vietnam war was getting increased publicity and I could foresee my son (then 13) going off to be killed or maimed. During that summer I was sharing and praying with a friend whose daughter had attempted suicide, and I'm sure my mental and emotional state was little better than hers at the time. Yet I was hoping against hope that somehow things would improve. Instead, the tension became so great in my body that I began to have pain in the back of my head. I endured it as I had so much other psychosomatic pain until I was forced to see my physician. I told him it was either a physical or spiritual problem; he ruled out the physical, leaving me with a spiritual problem of gigantic proportions. I had sought every place I knew for help and found none so I got my prescription for anti-anxiety/depression pills and joined an elite crowd of copout artists who exist on tranquilizers. I took the first bottle and found that the pain was kept under control. Occasionally, I would forget to take a pill to work for my noontime dose and would be unable to turn my head by the end of the day. Being no better, I proceeded to refill the prescription. I thought it was ridiculous for a Christian to live on pills, but there was no other recourse known to me.

I had asked God to search my heart for any hidden sin or unyielded area of my life, all to no avail. About this time a friend loaned me a copy of Alan Redpath's book, *Victorious Christian Living.* It was similar in message to Watchman Nee's *The Normal Christian Life,* which my dear friend, Dr. Raymond Buker, had supplied me two or three years earlier. I had read Nee's book several times without the conscious thought that such a life could be a reality for me. However, I'm certain the Holy Spirit used it more in my life than I had realized. As I read *Victorious Christian Living* daily for a while, I was getting closer to October 25, 1965 when God was to reveal a Scripture to me which I had memorized some years earlier . . . .

# "Crucified With Christ..."

Galatians 2:20

October 25, 1965 dawned pretty much the same as any other day; things were no blacker than usual! I got up and forced myself to a job that had not been fulfilling in fourteen years and there was little likelihood that this day would be anything but more of the same. There was one redeeming aspect — I had a supervisor, Bill Dowe (now owner of Heritage House Publications) and many other wonderful people as associates and friends in my work. I had great supervisors during my nearly nineteen-year-stay at Martin-Marietta Corporation and was never treated unfairly in all my time at the company. Without those challenging personal relationships the work itself could never have provided sufficient stimulation to have kept me going.

As the day wore on I found that I was not only depressed but the anxiety which had been channeled into physical manifestations was now surfacing. I felt as though I was shaking all over and that I would certainly lose my mind before the day had ended. But, dutifully, I put in the entire

101

eight hours, and the next major effort was to drive the car home. I didn't see how I could possibly do it, but I finally made it with the firm hope that I could get to bed as quickly as possible. I had some bad news in store for me; it was PTA meeting night and there was no way I could get out of going and sitting through a miniature of my son's seventh grade classes! Somehow I struggled through it and made it back home without blowing my mind. I knew I was in no condition to go to bed so I waited until my wife and children were in bed and then read something in the Word and continued reading where I had left off the night before in Redpath's book. I don't know how long I read; but, eventually, I came across Galatians 2:20: "I am crucified with Christ: [literally: have been] nevertheless I live; yet not I, but Christ liveth in me: and the life which I now live in the flesh I live by the faith of the Son of God, who loved me, and gave himself for me."

As I read this verse the reality of it was driven home by the Holy Spirit and I fell to my knees in the presence of God. In fact, it was so real that I even opened my eyes to see if He were visible. It was as though I was filled with the Spirit from head to foot; I literally tingled as the thrill of deliverance for which I had waited in unbelief was finally realized.

As I revelled in the joy of being freed from depression, anxiety, despair, loneliness, insecurity, feelings of inferiority and any other thing contrary to the peace that passes all understanding, my hand suddenly went to the back of my head. There was no pain! It was well past midnight when the thrill subsided sufficiently to go to bed. Then about 5 A.M. I awakened my wife to share with her what God had done, and we wept tears of joy together. It was destined to be three to five years later before she was to be able fully to appreciate the significance of my release from the self-life with all its shackles.

## JOURNEY TO THE END OF SELF

When I came to Jesus
   For the cleansing of my sin, (John 3:3)
My heart was set at peace
   As the Saviour came within. (2 Cor. 5:17)

Looking to His promise
   Of a life of victory, (2 Cor. 2:14)
My faith was sadly taxed
   As I struggled to be free. (Rom. 7:24,25)

The burdens that I bore
   Were heavier day by day;
It seemed God didn't care (Ps. 142:4)
   As I labored in the way.

I searched for other means
   For relief from trials sore;
No comfort could I find
   And I yielded to Him more. (Rom. 12:1)

My Lord had heard my cry; (Ps. 142)
   And began to guide my way; (Ps. 37:5)
Tho' comfort was not giv'n
   He refused to let me stray.

My strength was well nigh gone,
   And continued to decrease;
Until there was no more
   And He gave to me His peace. (John 14:27)

My heart was filled with peace
   That passeth understanding; (Phil. 4:6,7)
I knelt in heartfelt awe

My soul was not demanding.

Tho' pain had been my lot, (Phil. 1:29,30)
In His suffering I was blest; (Phil. 3:10)
Crucified with Christ, (Gal. 2:20)
I have found in Him my rest. (Matt. 11:28,29)

C. R. Solomon

As in previous dealings with the Lord and His with me, no one shared the perils of the victorious life which are equally as devastating as the joys are edifying. I wanted to remain totally open to the Spirit's working in my life, but I was unaware that I was equally open to satanic attack or demonic harassment. Within a week my mind was flooded with impure thoughts; it was almost two years later that I was to discover Satan's part in this and be freed from it.

I read voraciously in the Word and in books on spiritual growth in order to understand better this new-found freedom. As I did so, I knew that I couldn't live in the aura of one experience so I endeavored to understand my position in Christ. I read between 50 and 100 books that first year and began to put into focus my eighteen years of Christian experience and service prior to understanding the operation of the cross in my life. My life had not been unproductive since I had been involved in soul winning, Bible studies, etc. However, I found that I had been working out my problems on other people. I had known all along that I still had my problems but was powerless to do anything about them.

I still had no inkling as to God's way or what He was

bringing to pass. It gradually began to dawn on me that others who suffered from so-called "mental illness" were no different from what I had been except in degree. As I contemplated sharing the growth truths, it seemed logical that the best way would be in counseling. I had had considerable experience in soul winning and one to one relationships, so in the summer of 1967 I enrolled in the evening school at the University of Colorado in a beginning counseling course. My wife was open to my going to California that fall to take some intensive counseling training. While there, I heard of a pastor whom I knew that I must see immediately. While resting that evening prior to going to see him, the numerals 50:14 came into my mind. I was half asleep and dismissed it. During the mid-week Bible study I looked through my Bible and found Psalm 50:14: "Offer unto God thanksgiving; and pay thy vows unto the most High" and verse 15 adds: "And call upon me in the day of trouble: I will deliver thee, and thou shalt glorify me." That night as I shared with the pastor, I was freed from demonic obsession in my thought life.

A short time later while still in California, I was reading Isaiah 58 when the Holy Spirit drew my attention to verses 10 and 11: "And if thou draw out thy soul to the hungry, and satisfy the afflicted soul; then shall thy light rise in obscurity, and thy darkness be as the noon day; and the Lord shall guide thee continually, and satisfy thy soul in drought, and make fat thy bones: and thou shalt be like a watered garden, and like a spring of water, whose waters fail not."

No passage with which I am familiar could have been a more appropriate call to the ministry which I now knew to be an indisputable fact.

A month or so later, back in Denver, my sleep was interrupted by satanic emissaries. Upon resisting in that area and having my sleep restored, I was praying by a chair one night and a vase came off a bookcase and fell near me. If this had happened a few months previously I would have fled out the front door and left my wife and children to fend for themselves. Next came a satanic oppression which was worse than any depression I had ever known. I was unable to resist Satan so I requested prayer from others and the oppression lifted one night as I was reading Psalm 37. I discovered the "wicked" referred to in the Psalm was Satan who had been "spreading himself like a green bay tree."

The next day God gave me my first poem, "God's Processing Tunnel." By June, 1968, I had completed all of my basic counseling courses and the company needed a volunteer counselor in a program to train hardcore unemployed persons — a government program.

This counseling was the basis for my master's thesis.

In January, 1969, my attention was called to Deuteronomy 8:2: "And thou shalt remember all the way which the Lord thy God led thee these *forty years* in the wilderness, to humble thee, and to prove thee, to know what was in thine heart, whether thou wouldest keep his commandments, or not."

Later in the year, this number forty was to have great significance in God's leading regarding my employment.

Grace Fellowship International was incorporated May 29, 1969 with the express purpose of establishing a Christian counseling ministry. Mr. John A. Stevens and Dr. Raymond B. Buker and myself constituted the original board of directors of the non-profit corporation which was granted exempt status by Internal Revenue Service.

The Master of Personnel Service degree was awarded me by the University of Colorado in December 1969, and God made it clear to me, as will be later described in Chapter 8, that I was to leave the company in January, 1970, to begin the ministry.

Though there were no subsidizing individuals or groups, God supplied all needs as He had promised to do. Just before

I left the company He had given me a promise in Exodus 23:25: "And ye shall serve the Lord your God, and he shall bless thy bread, and thy water; and I will take sickness away from the midst of thee." After more than six years of counseling I have yet to miss a counseling appointment or to reschedule one because of sickness.

From the uncertainties of the beginning until the present my wife has stood by my side helping with secretarial work, bookkeeping and telephone counseling with contrary health conditions most of the time.

The beginnings of a world-wide ministry are well in view and it is all to the glory of Him who can make *something* out of *nothing.* "But God hath chosen the foolish things of the world to confound the wise; and God hath chosen the weak things of the world to confound things which are mighty; and base things of the world, and things which are despised, hath God chosen, yea, and things which are not, to bring to nought things that are: that no flesh should glory in his presence" (I Corinthians 1:27-29).

At this juncture I had three teenagers who had each been affected to one degree or another by my neurotic behavior in the family, and I suffered much guilt as I expected their lives to be ruined by their emotional and spiritual deprivation. Since this had all been a necessary part of my "boot camp," God gave me a promise about my children on March 24, 1968: "O thou afflicted, tossed with tempest, and not comforted, behold . . . all thy children shall be taught of the Lord; and great shall be the peace of thy children" (Isaiah 54:11a,13).

At this writing my two older children, Ronald and Catherine, are married; and the youngest, Susan, is in college.

# "...I Will Bring The Blind..."

Isaiah 42:16

Many persons come into the counseling office who have totally submitted their lives to the Lord by a volitional choice in the near or distant past. It has been helpful to many to understand God's commitment to their commitment. When months or years pass after the commitment with little or no positive change in the personality makeup or the circumstances, a person begins to question the validity of his commitment, or, worse yet, he questions God's ability to lead him after the commitment has been made.

Many times "Job's friends" come along and give him one or several methods for determining God's will. This makes about as much sense as an employee going on a job and trying everything to determine his supervisor's will for him instead of being available for the supervisor to tell him. As long as he is there, yielded and available for work, it is the supervisor's responsibility to communicate his will to him.

So it is in our relationship to our Lord. As we remain yielded and spend time in the Word and prayer getting to know Him, He communicates with us in a manner that enables us to understand His will in small or great matters.

The following diagram has been blessed of the Lord in some lives as they realized they were yet within the confines of God's will even though it seemed that all was lost.

The horizontal line represents God's perfect plan for a life, or the center of His will. Point #1 represents physical birth which is God's will or the individual would not exist. Point #2 represents rebirth which is also in God's will for a life since "He is not willing that any should perish, but that all should come to repentance" (II Peter 3:9). Point #3 represents total submission or total abandonment to the will of God in all areas of the life. Romans 12:1 states, "I beseech you therefore, brethren, by the mercies of God, that ye present your bodies a living sacrifice, holy, acceptable unto God, which is your reasonable service." It is not only His will but we are entreated to present voluntarily our lives to Him. Contingent upon that yielding is Romans 12:2, "And be not conformed to this world: but be ye transformed by the renewing of your mind, that ye may prove what is that good, and acceptable, and perfect, will of God." Being transformed by the renewing of our mind is not our work but His; once He has renewed our mind it is a relatively simple matter for Him to reveal His will to us.

Upon our submission to Him, it is as though he builds a wall behind us to prevent our going back on our commitment and two converging walls ahead of us to hedge us in to Himself. Sometimes we stay in the center of His will for a short time and then begin to stray, either willingly or ignorantly. Once we encounter the wall we learn that the direction we have taken is ill-advised, at best. We reverse and go in the other direction and overcorrect and overshoot His ideal for us. Nevertheless, He is faithful to chasten us, and the erected barricade on the other side nudges us back. After a few of those collisions with the wall we are more prone to

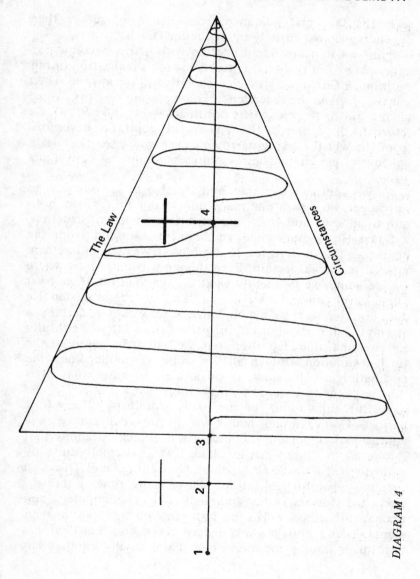

DIAGRAM 4

The Law

Circumstances

111

seek His face and guidance from His Word rather than depending almost entirely upon circumstances.

Point #4 indicates identification with Christ becoming an experiential reality. After entering into this realization of our position in Christ we stay closer to His will for a while. Then self often takes the ascendency and we again veer off. As we yield again to the cross (II Corinthians 4:11; Luke 9:23), we return to the center of His will. At this point, our deviations from His will for us are narrowing even when we must again be guided by circumstances represented by the converging walls.

As we approach the apex and are able to see our path in retrospect, we realize that many undesirable things from both our standpoint and God's are permitted for our instruction.

Since He is our guide and can see the end from the beginning, He is faithful to lead us if we will but remain yielded to His leadership. Even though we don't know where we are going, we frequently want to take the lead. If we trust our faithful Guide, all we need to know is the next step. He dare not give us the final objective or we would be certain to attempt a shortcut and fall into the morass! If we faithfully follow our Guide step after step, we will arrive safely at the final destination, though all the while we neither knew the destination nor the way. It sufficed us to know that He is "the way, the truth and the life" (John 14:6).

As the time came for me to leave industry, I saw how perfect God's timing had been in my deliverance, the educational opportunities, etc. I was forced to admit that during all of those years in which I was extremely unhappy with my lot, I was exactly where God wanted me! This is an extremely painful realization. Many, many times I thought God had forsaken me and that I had completely and permanently missed His purpose for putting me on this planet. Had I known I was hedged about and that God was faithful in leading me even when I was totally blind to His working in my life, what an encouragement it would have been in the midst of the depression.

"And I will bring the blind by a way that they knew not; I will lead them in paths that they have not known: I will make darkness light before them, and *crooked things straight.* These things will I do unto them, and not forsake them" (Isaiah 42:16).

HALLELUJAH!

# THE INS AND OUT OF REJECTION

# Dynamics
# of Distress

Since the inception of the ministry of Grace Fellowship International, it has been helpful to use the "wheel diagram" to depict the interactions between spirit, soul and body. While no graphic representation of man is without its shortcomings, visualization of spiritual truths can help some persons "see", by revelation of the Holy Spirit, the meaning of scriptural passages which had previously been only so many words.

In the following diagram, the soul is divided into its constituent functions, and the brain is depicted in the body such that the flow of data into the person and its subsequent dissemination into and out of the soul or personality may be traced. As will be noted, the process also works in the opposite direction with the flow of data emanating from within the personality. The brain, of course, is the control center for all bodily activity and is a physiological organ. The mind, by contrast, is a psychological phenomenon.

For purposes of clarity, the self-centered life with its

distress and the Christ-centered life with its freedom have been separated into succeeding chapters.

The shaded area at the periphery of the mind and emotions indicates that the functioning of the mind and emotions is largely unaffected by the Lord Jesus Christ coming into the life (represented by the "C" in the spirit) as long as He is not at the center or in control of the life. As depicted, the major areas of the mind and emotions are yet under the control of self (or flesh). A person thinks somewhat differently when he knows that his eternal destiny is settled. He may learn some Christian jargon and have a command of the cliches and even practice the behavior expected of the particular group with which he may fellowship. Also, the certainty of his new birth should take away the emotional fear of death. Beyond this, the person would function mentally and emotionally much as he did before conversion. The case records in the counseling office are replete with the histories of those who having been Christians for years, even some in the ministry, are still fighting the same emotional or mental disturbances they had prior to receiving Christ. Since it is God's command in Philippians 4:6 that we have no anxiety, and verse 7 promises the peace that passes understanding through Christ Jesus, it stands to reason that our emotional state should reflect His presence. The self-centered Christian is abnormal in God's economy. When the Word speaks of a believer and his resources in Christ, it is assumed that Christ is central in the life. However, the Christian who has appropriated Christ as his life today is the exception rather than the rule.

Diagram 5 depicts information coming to the person through the five senses (a) and being converted by the brain (which is the data processing unit) into information which can be handled by the mind. The incoming data is then referred to the mind (b) for interpretation. Depending upon the nature of the information, the emotions (c) may be involved to a small or great extent. The result of the

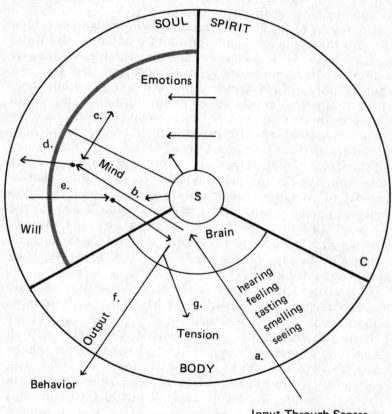

*DIAGRAM 5*

117

interaction of mind and emotions (d) must be brought to a decision, which is the function of the will. The decision may be made on the basis of emotion or logic or a combination of the two. Or, else, no decision is made indicating that the mental and emotional turmoil has interfered with the decision-making capability.

The results of the action (or inaction) in the will (e) is then fed into the brain for manifestation through the body. If the message to the brain is clear-cut and decisive, the behavior (f) is implemented immediately. If the program fed into the brain is more diffuse, some output will take place but some of the confused direction will be dumped into the body (g) in the form of tension. The tension usually localizes in some organ and gives rise to psychosomatic ailments such as headaches, nervous stomach, fatigue, etc.

As depicted by the arrows from the spirit to the soul, the Holy Spirit works through our spirit to affect our behavior and use us to some degree in spite of ourselves! There are many examples where God has greatly used a man in the ministry prior to the self-life being dealt with. D.L. Moody was one such man. He had held several successful evangelistic campaigns before he entered into the Spirit-filled or Spirit-controlled life.

The arrows from self to the mind and emotions indicate that self remains the final (though illegal) authority in most activity involving the individual.

It should be noted that a person with self or flesh controlling his existence is not free to be the unique human being God created him to be. It is as though his mind, will, and emotions are clogged so as to be unable to perform effectively in unison. When a person invites Christ into his life and deliberately (or through ignorance) maintains control, the stage is set for conflict or a power struggle. Some persons who were well-adjusted prior to conversion begin to experience internal conflict afterward. When the right of the

Lord Jesus Christ to control the life is disputed, the Romans 7 experience is the result.

Diagram 6 shows some of the feelings of inferiority and insecurity, most of which are developed through experiencing rejection along with being alienated from God's love. The brain, acting in the role of a computer or data processing unit, must have a program fed into it before it can be expected to function. The emotions and mind have their individual programs developed through all of the experiences which have been the lot of the individual. The body has been created by God to have innate drives (1) such as hunger, thirst, sex, etc., which form a type of physiological program which must be integrated with that of the mind and emotions.

All of the foregoing is separate and apart from the fact that the inner man or the spirit has another program (2) from within, and sin (and its author, Satan) attempts to implement a program (3) from without. In this chapter the psychological conflict of the self-centered life is the subject being treated; in Chapter 6 the spiritual conflict will be treated which also provides the key to freedom from psychological turmoil.

Now that we have the picture before us, let's look at some of the dynamics of the self-centered life as the conflict develops.

Beginning with the feelings of inferiority and insecurity, the mind must consider (a) the validity of such feelings. Frequently, the reasoning goes, "I feel inferior; therefore, I must *be* inferior!" Based upon this reasoning (b) the Will makes a choice or judgment. When the decision is handed down (c), the "inferior" program is implemented and the result is inferior behavior or performance. The behavior evokes a response on the part of others which creates a variety of adverse circumstances and the resulting input or feedback (4) is another variable to be integrated into the system. When self is unable to cope satisfactorily with the

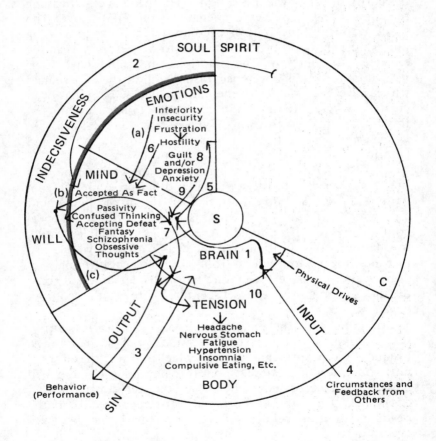

*DIAGRAM 6*

new input, the result (5) is frustration which breeds hostility.

As this new data is interpreted by the mind (6), the Will must make a choice to contain the hostility or dump it on some external person, animal or thing. Taking out the hostility (7) externally may well result in negative feedback which, in turn, causes guilt (8). When the decision (or indecision) results in internalizing the hostility the result is depression and anxiety (9). Displaced hostility causes problems for *others* and displaced anxiety causes trouble or tension (10) within *us*. Such tension which continues unabated over time gives rise to psychosomatic ailments of various descriptions.

When the mind can no longer handle the internal and external stress, it can resort to distorting or even denying reality and shifting responsibility or blame to others. A person who *distorts* reality is described as neurotic; when he *denies* reality he is diagnosed as psychotic. Someone has said that a neurotic person builds castles in the air; a psychotic person lives in them; and a psychiatrist collects the rent!

Some persons are more prone to fight their problems in their minds while others have more conflict in their emotions. Those who wrestle with their problems emotionally sometimes deliberately try to "flip out" or avoid reality in a vain attempt to escape the pain. Some have admitted this in counseling but could not make it work for them.

Those who are constituted to do mental gymnastics can very easily take a flight from reality through fantasy or psychotic delusions. Some can make it work so well that they have no apparent anxiety at all.

Even though it is rather undignified and lacking in sophistication from the vantage point of the psychiatrist or psychologist, depression could be defined in simple terms as an internal tantrum centered primarily in the emotions. Likewise, the person who is more prone to handle his inner conflicts in his mind could be said to have a "mental tantrum" which is usually labelled as "mental illness." Since the problem is apparently in the mind or in the emotions psychological treatment or therapy of some sort is usually the order of the day. Thus, the symptoms are treated and may be overcome in varying degrees but the basic conflict remains untouched.

Some adults will act out their tantrums phsycially and childishly when self doesn't get its way, but most are somewhat more subtle about it. It is like a parent giving a child in a tantrum its way. The symptoms subside immediately! However, the basic problem, the self-centered life, is worsened since the child has now found an effective way of manipulating his environment.

Likewise, when therapy is performed which reduces the emotional and/or mental symptoms, the manifestation of the tantrum subsides but the self (or flesh) has now learned an effective way to manipulate the environment.

A parent isn't doing a child a favor when he gives in to self-centered behavior and thus, reinforces or rewards negative behavior. This same child in adult life will resort to very similar behavior and will usually find a willing therapist who acts in the parents' stead and treats the symptoms instead of the self life. Since neither the parent nor the therapist faces the "person in tantrum" with the real issue, self or flesh, the person in need experiences a type of rejection. He has unknowingly asked for bread and has unwittingly been given a stone. He needs an answer consistent with truth but is given one which denies, either tacitly or verbally, that self or flesh is the problem.

Treatment of symptoms is of help and somewhat comforting on a temporary basis. If symptomatic treatment is continued too long a person could very well die of the disease. Consider for a moment a person who has a high fever due to pneumonia. A sympathetic friend could help some by bathing the person with cool water or giving an alcohol rubdown and thereby reduce the fever. If no other treatment such as antibiotics were provided to get to the source of the problem, the person might eventually be very cool — dead!

When neither the behavior nor the treatment results in resolution of internal and external conflict since it isn't dealing with reality — the reality of the self-life and Christ the ultimate Reality — the result is increased frustration. Thus, the feedback or input through the senses, the brain, and then the mind provides an unending source of irritation. The mind becomes more confused and passive; and as it does, the decisions made by the will are increasingly self-defeating. The resultant emotional conflict is more and more sustained in the organism and dumped into the body. When the physical resources are depleted and there has yet to be established a *functional* relationship with the Lord Jesus Christ where spiritual resources can be drawn upon, a physical and/or psychological breakdown occurs.

Human therapy can teach one to cope with and assuage some symptoms for varying lengths of time. The only permanently satisfying answer is to be found in the therapy of the Holy Spirit as He applies the cross to the self-life.

## SUMMARY

A progressive summary of the interactions within the soul might appear as follows:

Feelings of inferiority and insecurity
Withdrawal or compensation
Emotional Frustration
Hostility
   a. Outward Reaction
    (possibly accompanied by increased guilt)
   b. Inward Reaction
    (1) depression and anxiety
    (2) tension

(3)  psychosomatic ailments

Reality Distortion (By mind for relief)
    a. Deny Reality
    b. Blame others

Copout by claiming to be "mentally ill"
Increased guilt and frustration
Ultimate breakdown
(Physically and/or psychologically)

# The Perils of the Well-adjusted

The previous chapter has been slanted toward the Christian who is emotionally or mentally unstable since these are the persons who are forced to look for answers to their problems (or symptoms). But the well-adjusted fleshly Christian has a more devastating problem because he usually doesn't realize he has a problem! He may not be aware that he is operating in the strength of self or that a much better way is available. Since his love for the Lord and lack of neuroticism permits him unhindered use of his soul strength or natural ability, he is called upon for service and positions of leadership. A greater percentage of Christian service or ministry than most would like to admit is performed by just such persons. Usually, this person is recognized as a "mature" Christian. A professional person such as a physician finds himself in double jeopardy! He may have only been saved yesterday; but he finds his opinions, even though he may be merely thinking aloud, taken as profound pronouncements of truth. Many who are lacking in spiritual discernment and who have been trained to think the doctor is always right will accept the logic of a good mind and human wisdom as being directed by the Holy Spirit.

When we refer to "gifted" people we generally mean a superior mental ability, a characteristic of the soul or a natural talent such as musical ability which has no connection with a person's knowing the Lord Jesus Christ. Although these soulical gifts are not to be discounted, the distinction between these and spiritual gifts must be maintained. The person who is to perform a spiritual ministry must be exercising a spiritual gift if the work is to prosper and be blessed of the Lord.

The following are some suggestions of areas for consideration by the well-adjusted person as a check-up to see if he is operating in self (after the flesh) or in the Spirit. Remember, a person does not need to be a psychological basket case for self to be a controlling menace. The neurotic person may do such damage to himself, but the well-adjusted person in a position of leadership may propagate a malady and do much damage to others thereby affecting many generations.

## THE WELL-ADJUSTED SYNDROME

In considering the well-adjusted person it will be primarily from the standpoint of Christian service since such a person is rarely seen in the counseling office until later in life when he has been caught in the crucible of testing.

When such a person submits to psychological testing he comes out with flying colors; some Christian organizations are deceived by this and rely heavily on these results in selecting personnel. Since the tests by definition are measurements in the area of the soul or personality, no estimate can be given as to the degree to which the Holy Spirit will override or utilize personality weaknesses.

The Holy Spirt does not need to call those who are

endowed by natural ability to perform a particular ministry. This could too easily tempt a person to take credit for the accomplishment and rob God of the glory. His call of the individual is based on His sovereign will, and any suffering of mental and emotional symptoms may be part of his "boot camp" or preparation for the Lord's army.

When those who have "personality problems" are rejected for missionary service or other ministry in favor of a well-adjusted person, the loss to the Lord's work may be incalculable. In interviewing many missionary candidates it has been the author's experience that those with the most severe hangups are the most ready to face their need and appropriate their resources in Christ. Such a person is uniquely prepared to face the rigors of the mission field since he is not depending upon his own strength or others or cultural props to sustain him. The well-adjusted fleshly Christian, on the other hand has not been forced to rely on the Lord and little realizes the extent to which he utilizes his resourcefulness in a friendly culture to meet his needs and perform his ministry.

The deception which has been perpetrated by the Enemy has resulted in a great percentage of persons being launched into a "spiritual" ministry who are well-adjusted psychologically but who are adjusted spiritually to a fleshly model. The educational procedure in too many Bible schools and seminaries emphasizes the training of the mind and assumes that assimilation or spiritual growth has kept pace. It is possible to articulate material studied in formal training or in private study without the truths having become experiential.

It is not an exaggeration to state that a substantial majority of Bible colleges and seminaries have no systematic counseling program where each individual's spiritual growth can be assessed on a continuous basis during his formal training. As a result too many graduates go out into the ministry filled with themselves instead of the Holy Spirit teaching truths which they themselves have not experienced.

Religious flesh is just as detestable in the sight of God as irreligious flesh, if not more so. Religious flesh tends to self-righteousness and pride which is specifically condemned in the Word. The fact that self or flesh is in control of the life indicates that God (the Holy Spirit) has been replaced at the helm of the life. Anything or any person displacing and replacing God is an idol, so the person who is allowing self or flesh to control is an idolator. And idolatry is specifically named as sin.

The well-adjusted Christian is usually able to function in positions of leadership and ministry for long periods of time before it becomes apparent that spiritual ministry is lacking. This is true since the majority of those evaluating his efforts are also walking after the flesh. Those who would dare to make a spiritual assessment under the leading of the Holy Spirit may be accused of being judgmental and divisive and prevented from participating in leadership. Thus, spiritual discernment is disregarded by fleshly attitudes and a carnal majority rules!

Since the flesh is of the world, it follows that the methodology of the world system would be adopted or practiced to some extent in the operation of the church. It is exceedingly popular to borrow from the world system and "Christianize" that which works for the world. This has been true for education and is also true for counseling. The method the Lord Jesus used in teaching was to show the disciples how to do it and later explain the principles or the theology, if you will. We generally teach the theology and then the practice, if indeed the practice is taught at all. In the area of counseling, much of what is taught in seminaries has been borrowed from the world-system developments, couched in scriptural terminology and proffered as "Christian counseling." Some seminary students are taught in the setting of a mental institution by those trained in psychotherapy.

When this is done, both the Word and psychotherapy are watered down to the point where neither is effective.

There could be many other areas explored where the fleshly Christian adapts or adopts the world system and gets some mileage out of it to the detriment of those looking to him for true spiritual and biblical ministry. The minister and consequently those ministered to have been given the impression that it is necessary to be thoroughly trained by the world-system or its equivalents to be effective in understanding people and helping them. As a result the minister frequently has an inferiority complex and refers people for "professional help" when he is in the profession which should be doing the helping.

Trusting the Holy Spirit to do all that needs to be done in the life or in the ministry presupposes total dependence upon Him which is foreign to the well-adjusted fleshly Christian. So long as he yet has some confidence in his own abilities and training he will be unable to "forsake all that he has" and follow the Lord. Until he does he is not filled or controlled by the Spirit which is the prerequisite given in the Word for those called of the Lord and commissioned for spiritual service. True spiritual strength follows hard on the heels of recognition of spiritual bankruptcy. Unless and until such be the case, most of the efforts of the well-adjusted, fleshly Christian may be designated as *work for the Lord* rather than *ministry in the Spirit.*

Those points for consideration which follow are overlapping and are far from being exhaustive.

## TALENTS MISTAKEN FOR SPIRITUAL GIFTS

Believers are frequently exhorted to "use their talents" for the Lord. This may, or may not, be of the Lord. A fleshly Christian with a technically perfect singing voice might perform flawlessly with no spiritual message whatever other than that transmitted by the lyrics of the song. Many such persons sing "for the Lord" but the compliments they receive pander to their pride and they revel in the attention they receive. When this is the case they are in the place of prominence rather than the Lord and they receive the glory, not Him. Similarly, a man who is a good orator with a quick mind and a pleasing personality could deceive himself and others into thinking he is God's gift to the church as a minister. Although a big splash may be made initially, over the long haul the spiritual results do not substantiate his claim to his calling until such time as the flesh comes under the cross.

## PERSUASIVE ARGUMENTATION SUBSTITUTED FOR THE SPIRIT'S CONVINCING

Preaching which is designed to elicit an emotional response may do just that. Good oratory and well-placed human interest stories may play on the emotions of the listeners and result in moving them to some kind of action. Arousal of false guilt may be evoked rather than the Spirit's conviction of sin. Extended appeals for decisions may result in an *external show* without the *internal glow* as evidenced by the instability and failure to "follow through" on the part of many of those making decisions. The emotional response on the part of the person in the pew is sometimes mistaken for a spiritual decision when the results are tallied.

Decisions made out of false guilt on the part of the person in the pew are not fostered by the Holy Spirit and, hence, no spiritual issues are settled. This being the case, the person may have embarked on an endless merry-go-round of answering altar calls to prove his sincerity to the Lord. When his needs are not met, he may eventually conclude that God has also rejected him and become embittered toward God and the church when neither is responsible for the predicament. Altar workers are too frequently lacking in training and the necessary time to deal with the individual to determine the difference between false or psychological guilt and the convicting work of the Holy Spirit. Some persons go to the altar so frequently that they feel guilty if they don't!

A strong personality on a committee or board can convince some others to go along with *him* when that may be all they are doing. Those in the group who feel inferior and lacking in acceptance are unlikely to oppose such strength.

## GRAVITATION TO POSITIONS OF LEADERSHIP

Many in church and denominational leadership are there on the basis of a good mind, a strong will and good politics rather than being placed there by the Holy Spirit. Such men become despots and those under them learn that disagreement with them is likely to draw fire instead of prayer. They eventually become defensive of their position and are concerned about promotion to the next higher position. If they are passed over there is hostility instead of humility; they are more concerned with ruling than acting as a servant. Being deposed from a position of leadership might well result in the establishment of a rival movement rather than unstinting support and prayer for the replacement.

## CLASHING OPINIONS RATHER THAN UNITY IN THE SPIRIT

When attempting to arrive at and implement decisions by power rather than prayer, it is not surprising that church fights and splits over minor issues are not infrequent. The watching world has every right to assume that Christians do not love one another when they observe such happenings.

## ENTHUSIASM MISTAKEN FOR SPIRITUAL MOTIVATION

Much enthusiasm stems from a fleshly desire to succeed so as to gratify self. Spiritual motivation, on the other hand, might be less flashy and could appear to be passivity in the world's view.

## MULTITUDINOUS IDEAS SPAWNED BY
## A FLESHLY MIND

The "try this and that" approach to see what works may have some results but those who wait on the Lord will have fewer false starts and more permanent and eternal results.

### SELF-CONFIDENCE FOSTERS INDEPENDENCE

A person who has considerable talent and strength acts as though he is self-sufficient in many situations. Therefore, he is not forced to rely completely upon the Lord and often is uncooperative with others. When suggestions or constructive criticism are offered, it is taken as a threat to his competence; acceptance of a contrary opinion would indicate weakness and is often declined even though obviously the wise path.

### TACIT INSISTENCE UPON "CREDIT" FOR
### SUCCESS OF IDEAS, PROGRAMS, OR PROJECTS

If credit goes to others for the successful outcome of a project, such a person is likely to withdraw and start something where he will be in the limelight and benefit more from his own efforts.

### HAPPINESS MISTAKEN FOR THE JOY OF THE LORD

Happiness is a soulical or psychological state whereas joy is a fruit of the Spirit. A person who is happy by nature may fold up under the trials of life in the long run or under the pressure of a foreign culture. If all the cultural props and personal relationships are intact, he prospers. But when he encounters a situation such as a foreign field where he must depend almost solely upon his spiritual resources, he is at a loss. If he is on a foreign field, he either has a breakdown or personality conflicts make it impossible for others to work with him. Frequently he can blame it on his wife's "health problems" since she has to absorb his hostility as well as her own.

## COURAGE MISTAKEN FOR BOLDNESS IN THE SPIRIT

Courage arising from self-confidence, which results in being impervious to the criticisms of others might lead to impetuous and rash behavior, whereas holy boldness would be more quiet and unobtrusive.

## INTOLERANCE FOR NEUROTIC PERSONS

The well-adjusted person usually finds it very difficult to understand and be empathic with those who are severely neurotic. Since he has never been in that condition, he regards it as weakness which the person could overcome in his own strength if he simply made the choice and applied himself.

## RAILING AGAINST OTHERS WITH DOCTRINAL DIFFERENCES

Although heresy and false doctrine are not to be countenanced, those in error are to be treated in love and scripturally shown the truth. They are to be entreated as brothers, not rejected as enemies because their beliefs and/or practice does not measure up to scriptural injunctions. Most church splits and denominational splinters are not over the fundamentals of the faith but over lack of fundamental faith.

## USE OF PROGRAMS, ORGANIZATION, PROMOTION, FINANCES, AND PEOPLE AS A SUBSTITUTE FOR SPIRITUAL POWER

A man with much *charisma* (personality strength) may develop what seems to be a solid work for the Lord. The acid test that proves whether the work is of man or the Spirit is faced when he is removed from leadership. If it is of the Lord and organized around scriptural principles it will continue and flourish; if it is of man, it will take a nose dive before it is rebuilt under new leadership.

This type of work is built around a man whereas

scripturally sound works are organized around the Man, the Lord Jesus Christ. Then, when God calls the organizer to another place of ministry or home to Heaven, God's choice of a replacement will not need to try to be someone he isn't.

## BODY TENSIONS GO UNRECOGNIZED OR IGNORED UNTIL A MENTAL OR PHYSICAL BREAKDOWN OCCURS

A person who is strong physically and psychologically may carry great loads and overloads for long periods of time. Since he apparently takes it all in his stride, he gradually assumes more and more responsibility. In doing so he harms himself because of the cumulative cost, and he robs others of the chance to grow in the Lord and in administrative skills.

There is a saying that goes, "It is settled by natural law how much a good horse can draw." Although a person is strong physically there may be generalized tension as he assumes much of the responsibility that the Lord should be carrying. What results? One day this person, who seemingly doesn't have a care in the world and is the picture of health, has an early coronary and is removed from the scene.

The devastation to himself, should he survive, to his family and to the work he headed is all the greater since he took to himself a weight of responsibility that God never intended him to bear in his own strength.

# Dynamics of Deliverance

Note: Please read the "Important Note" in the Preface to Part Two before proceeding with this chapter.

The very title of the Chapter connects being delivered *from* something *to* something. Up to this point we have considered being delivered from slavery to sin, and terms such as self and flesh have been utilized without sufficient definition for the person who has not been steeped in theological jargon. Prior to beginning a discussion of the spiritual and psychological dynamics involved when a person enters into victory through identification with Christ, some definitions must be considered.

A common misconception among Christians, nay the public generally, is that the soul has some spiritual attributes. The preface to a recent psychological text contributed the information that psychologists do not work in the realm of the soul, proving that Christians are not the only ones who are confused. In earlier chapters the soul has been described as consisting of the functions of intellect, emotions, and volition which just happen to be the same as that for personality. Thus, we conclude that soul and personality are synonomous; and these will be used interchangeably.

This brings us to another term which bears some clarification — self. There is a spiritual use of the term as well as a psychological application. Each of us is a unique self due to the inherent personality traits with which we are endowed by birth and as modified and developed by subsequent interaction with our environment. This self is the same as that possessed by an animal and is neither "good" or "bad" from a moral standpoint. And, it goes without saying that this self is not the one to which the cross is applied.

When we speak of self at the center of the life, we are using the word with a spiritual connotation. At other times it is used as an adjective describing a quality of existence, the self-life. The King James Version uses a term, flesh, which means the same as self in certain instances. Flesh is connected with sins and is in antithesis to the Spirit or that which God would accomplish in and through us (Galatians 5:17).

To go back one step further, it is necessary to consider such terms as sin nature, Adamic nature, old man, old nature, old self, etc. These are all used by theologians or in various translations of the Bible. The most complete models of man for explaining man's makeup and functioning have been devised by secular men and have given little, if any, credence to man's spiritual nature. Theologians on the other hand, have delved into systematic theology and like endeavors to the point that the foreground has almost gone underground! However, models of man which are truly functional and which thoroughly integrate the spiritual and the psychological are sadly lacking. Because of this, some of the theological definitions are incomplete and do not lend themselves to functional usage.

There are cases when a definition is accepted for one term

that several other definitions or corollaries go along with the package. It is either/or with nothing in between. Such is the controversy over the old man or old nature (old self, NIV) and the effect which the new birth has on it. If we take the view that the sin nature is put out of business, we are automatically expected and said to teach sinless perfection, or entire sanctification. If we say it has been put out of business positionally, we are put in the camp of teaching progressive sanctification. These two views are usually considered to be mutually exclusive. It is the goal of this book to strike a balance between positional sanctification, critical (crisis) sanctification and progressive sanctification.

Since the author has never formally studied theology, perhaps the reader will grant him the leeway to enter another way of looking at sanctification as pertains to the power of sin into the arena for consideration, even though it has probably been posed by a dozen people each century since Christ was on planet Earth.

## HYPOTHESIS

*It was Adam's death to God, spiritually, that caused his "old man" to come into existence or come alive toward Satan which rendered him a servant to sin; to reverse the process through redemption, it was necessary for the "old man" to die to Satan and sin and that man's spirit come alive (be regenerated) to God in order for man to become a servant of righteousness.*

On the basis of the above, the old man is synonomous with the dead spirit, the sin nature, the Adamic nature, the old self, etc. Adam died spiritually because of sin and became a servant of sin unto death; in redemption, the "old man" is crucified with Christ that the redeemed sinner might become a servant of obedience unto righteousness (Romans 6:16). This would sound as though it would be impossible to sin; but this can not be supported by scripture nor by the

137

experience of New Testament or present-day Christians. The works of the flesh are attributed to *both the saved and unsaved;* but what is the flesh?

According to the hypothesis, the "old man" or old nature has been rendered inoperative by crucifixion so sins do not emanate from this source. Sin, empowered by Satan, formerly exercised its evil deeds through the co-operation of the "old man" and thereby enslaved the personality or soul; the Christian has had his "old man" rendered inoperative through the cross but permits through ignorance, deceit, or volitional choice the power of sin to dominate his personality – this latter condition is herein described by the word *flesh*.

The New International Version (Zondervan) translates this usage of flesh as the "sinful nature" and differentiates between this and the "old self". Thus, the "old self" would be the KJV equivalent of the "old man" and would be that entity inherited from Adam which was crucified in and with Christ. The "old man" or "old self" was crucified with Christ whether or not the believer avails himself of the freedom from the power of sin or not. This judicial and positional crucifixion (positional sanctification) can be appropriated by faith (critical sanctification) and based on such appropriation the believer can reckon (or count) himself dead to the control of sin but alive unto (the control of) God through the Lord Jesus Christ (Romans 6:11), continuously (progressive sanctification).

Thus, the contradistinction is made between the "old man", Adamic nature, sin nature, or "old self" and the "flesh", self, or "sinful nature". The former might be thought of as *the necessity* to sin whereas the latter might be a *propensity to sin* or the *capability of responding to sin.*

The crucifixion of the "old man" does not render the Christian sinless but gives him the freedom of choice to serve sin or to serve righteousness – to walk after the flesh (self or sinful nature) or to walk after the Spirit.

Now, it behooves us to make another clarification. The KJV makes a distinction between *being* in the flesh and walking or living *after* the flesh. There may not be sufficient warrant from the Greek to build a solid case on prepositions, but this difference is hereby taken as an assumption: The natural man is *in* the flesh and has no other alternative but to walk or live *in* the flesh and *after* the flesh. Romans 8:6 states "So then they that are in the flesh cannot please God." This would seem to be the same thought as that of Hebrews 11:6a, "But without faith it is impossible to please Him . . ." Romans 8:9 goes on to say, "But ye are not in the flesh but in the Spirit if so be that the Spirit of God dwell in you. Now if any man have not the Spirit of Christ, he is none of his." These two passages would seem to make it clear that we are either *in* the flesh or *in* the Spirit. The Christian, then, is *in* the Spirit but he may walk *after* the flesh or, to put it another way, he may live as though he is dead!

To summarize, the natural or unsaved man is *in* the flesh and walks or lives *in* and *after* the flesh. The Christian is *in* the Spirit and may walk or live *in* and *after* the Spirit, in which case he is termed a "spiritual" man; or he may walk or live *after* the flesh and be known as a carnal or fleshly man.

Another term which is assigned a specific meaning is the word, *death*. We speak of both physical and spiritual death, and these have one thing in common — separation from the source of life; this general meaning of death will be that utilized in the following discussion.

With the terminology defined in brief, let's turn to the application of the identification truths to the life of the individual. It is important to affirm again that our position or standing in Christ is perfect at the time of the new birth. The appropriation of the freedom gained through knowing experientially our identification or union with Christ is not a second work which the Holy Spirit does, it is entering into the victory made possible when we were baptized into the

Lord Jesus Christ by the Holy Spirit at regeneration. Romans 8:29 states that God's purpose for the believer is that he be conformed to the image of the Lord Jesus Christ. The condition or state of our walk involves both crises and process as we look at it in terms of sanctification. Progressive sanctification has our perfect state or standing (positional sanctification) as its goal with both crises and process being involved in the conforming of our lives to the image of the Lord Jesus Christ — our perfect position being progressively appropriated as our condition with the possibility of some crisis points along the way. A crisis might be defined as a discrete event at a point in time to differentiate it from necessarily having emotional dimensions.

In summary, we will study the dynamics of appropriating Christ as Life, both initially and on a continuing basis.

As we return to the analogy of a computer in describing the dynamics of deliverance, there is also some terminology peculiar to computer science that needs clarification. Many of the operations taking place within the human being have their counterparts in computer technology hence, the term "electronic brain".

The brain functions as a data processing unit. It knows nothing in and of itself and is totally dependent upon input, from without and within. This information within would correspond to a program which is fed into a computer. There is one type of program in the mind and yet another kind in the emotions. Either may take precedence and the operator, the will, chooses or permits a program or combination of programs and the resultant information is fed into the brain (Data Processing Unit) for implementation into behavior or performance.

Though there are an infinite variety of programs, there are ultimately only two programmers (the one who designs the program) in the Christian — either the flesh (self) or the Spirit (Christ). However, the flesh gets some choice help from the World and the Devil. The operator, the will, must make the choice concerning the source of the program to be employed. The programmers, flesh and Spirit, are in conflict one with the other. "For the flesh lusteth against the Spirit, and the Spirit against the flesh: and these are contrary the one to the other: so that ye cannot do the things that ye would" (Galatians 5:17). As the operator (will) makes the proper choice, the Holy Spirit supplies the power: "This I say then, (choose to) Walk in the Spirit, and ye shall not fulfill the lust of the flesh" (Galatians 5:16).

In other words the *will* makes the choice of the power source; the programmer or power source chosen determines the output or behavior — either the works of the flesh or the fruit of the Spirit (Galatians 5:19-23). Before continuing with the computer model it might be well to consider the power source and flow through the human being.

Diagrams 7, 8, 9, and 10 depict Adam before the Fall, the natural or unregenerate man, the carnal or fleshly man, and the spiritual or victorious man, respectively. Each diagram illustrates the source of power, the flow of power, the components involved, and the results.

Diagram 7 depicts Adam prior to his yielding to sin. He was in perfect communion with God or, as it is generally put, in a state of innocence. Sin was without, embodied in the Serpent, begging entry, but Adam was oblivious to it and willingly accepted directions from God who had made arrangements for his needs to be met in an ideal environment. His spirit, soul and body functioned in perfect unison. When Adam sinned he died spiritually just as God had told him he would. Diagram 8 shows the entry of sin and the dead spirit which resulted. From this point onward Adam and his progeny were constituted natural or unregenerated man as depicted in Diagram 8.

The will is the key of life. We have life and death set before us and our choices throughout our earthly pilgrimage

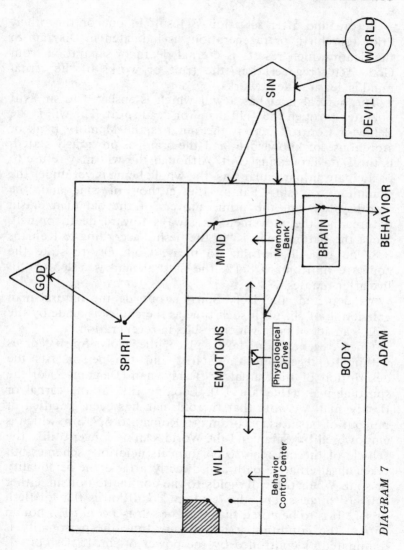

*DIAGRAM 7*

— before and after salvation — result in one or the other. Prior to rebirth or regeneration, as indicated in Diagram 8, the death which results is eternal death or separation from God. After regeneration, the fruit or works of the carnal mind is death — dead works.

The natural man has a will which is enslaved to sin as it operates through the "old man" or dead spirit. The will is the Behavior Control Center; the mind is the Memory Bank or storehouse of knowledge; and the brain, as previously stated, is the Data Processing Unit. Although the will may refuse to participate in particular sins, the whole being is yet under the dominion of sin. Satan, the author of sin, and the world-system are the prime movers of the old man or sin nature and the movement is always toward death or hell. Since the natural man is "in the flesh," according to Romans 8:8, he can do nothing to please God. Or, to state the converse of Romans 8:12, the natural man is a debtor "to live after the flesh."

As depicted, the Holy Spirit is outside the natural man convicting of sin until such time as the choice is made by the will — an act of faith which results in regeneration.

Once regeneration takes place the Holy Spirit comes within to regenerate the spirit, and the person fits the description of the carnal or fleshly man (Diagram 9) or the spiritual man (Diagram 10). Looking first at the carnal or fleshly man we note that the old man has been crucified or put out of business, according to Romans 6:6,7. Sin, which is empowered by Satan and the World, can no longer utilize the vehicle of the old man to perform its nefarious schemes but takes an alternative path and directly attacks the personality or soul. When the will yields to the domination of sin, either actively or passively, the resultant condition is that of flesh or self. It is to be noted that flesh or self is a *condition* not an *entity;* the condition exists at any time the personality is dominated or controlled by the power of sin. If flesh or self

144

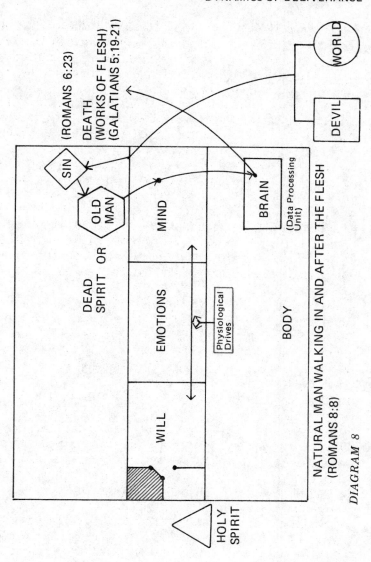

NATURAL MAN WALKING IN AND AFTER THE FLESH
(ROMANS 8:8)

*DIAGRAM 8*

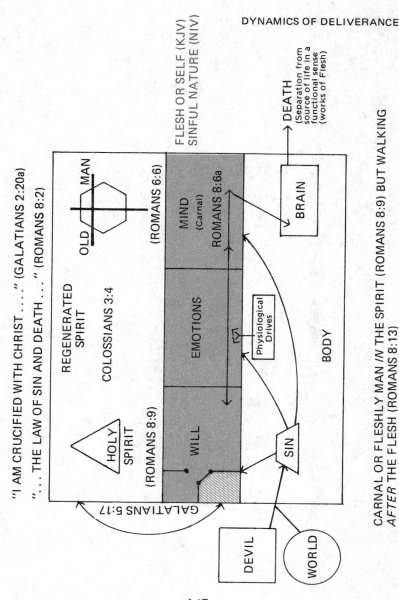

"I AM CRUCIFIED WITH CHRIST . . . ." (GALATIANS 2:20a)

". . . THE LAW OF SIN AND DEATH . . ." (ROMANS 8:2)

FLESH OR SELF (KJV)
SINFUL NATURE (NIV)

OLD MAN

REGENERATED SPIRIT

COLOSSIANS 3:4

(ROMANS 8:9)

HOLY SPIRIT

(ROMANS 6:6)

MIND
(Carnal)
ROMANS 8:6a

EMOTIONS

Physiological Drives

WILL

SIN

BODY

BRAIN

DEATH
(Separation from source of life in a functional sense (works of Flesh))

GALATIANS 5:17

DEVIL

WORLD

CARNAL OR FLESHLY MAN *IN* THE SPIRIT (ROMANS 8:9) BUT WALKING *AFTER* THE FLESH (ROMANS 8:13)
*DIAGRAM 9*

# THE INS AND OUT OF REJECTION

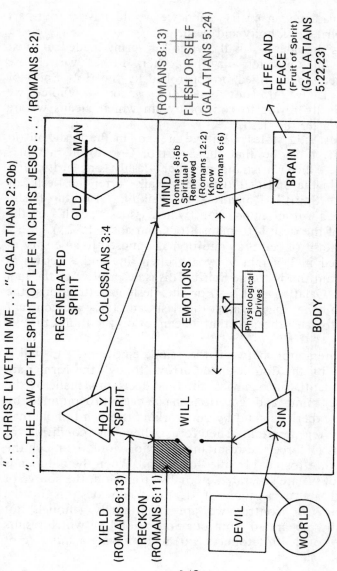

"... CHRIST LIVETH IN ME ..." (GALATIANS 2:20b)

"... THE LAW OF THE SPIRIT OF LIFE IN CHRIST JESUS ..." (ROMANS 8:2)

SPIRITUAL MAN — WALKING IN AND AFTER THE SPIRIT (GALATIANS 5:16)

DIAGRAM 10

149

were considered an entity, then we would have a four-part being: spirit, soul, body and flesh.

It is as though the "Will Switch" is spring loaded; it must stay in one position or the other. Either we choose deliberately to be filled or controlled by the Holy Spirit or sin; or, if we do not consciously make a choice we automatically revert to control by sin which means we are walking "after the flesh."

Romans 8:9a states, "But ye are not in the flesh, but in the Spirit, if so be that the Spirit of God dwell in you." Therefore, the Christian, whether fleshly or spiritual, is *always* "in the Spirit" but he may walk "after the flesh" or "after the Spirit" (Romans 8:4). Walking "after the flesh" produces a carnal mind from which issues "death" or the "works of the flesh" (Romans 8:6; Galatians 5:19-21).

Since flesh or self is a condition as opposed to an entity, it is depicted in Diagram 9 by a broken line and is shown as being in antithesis to the Spirit. This is descriptive of the fact stated in Galatians 5:17, "For the flesh lusteth against the Spirit, and the Spirit against the flesh: and these are contrary the one to the other: so that ye cannot do the things that ye would."

The interaction between the mind, emotions, and will is indicated by the double-ended arrow; though the former are both influential in behavior, the final decision is made by the will. The mind and emotions have been programmed by previous experience and by sin working through the old man prior to regeneration. Therefore, when the condition of "flesh" is in force the resultant behavior would be much the same as that fostered by the "old man." When the old man is in control we are separated eternally from God, the source of Life and are in a state of death. When flesh is in the ascendancy or control we are functionally (though not organically) separated from our Source of Life which results in a *state* of death (Romans 8:6) while having a *standing* of

Life (Colossians 3:4).

Though the old man has been crucified once and for all at Calvary as a sovereign act of God contingent upon our receiving Christ by faith, the "flesh with the affections and lusts" (Galatians 5:24) or the "deeds of the body" must be continuously mortified or brought to the place of death. This is accomplished as we choose (with our will) to "Walk in the Spirit, and ye shall not fulfill the lust of the flesh" (Galatians 5:16). In other words, when we choose to abide in Christ who is our life the personality cannot be empowered by sin which produces the condition known as flesh; when the flesh is not energized by its "life source," sin, it is effectually "dead" or has been brought under the working of the cross. The believer has mortified or brought to the place of death (Romans 8:13) the deeds of the body otherwise known as the "works of the flesh." The Christian has then chosen Life instead of death.

In all three diagrams an arrow is shown from the body into the arrow connecting mind, will and emotions indicating the physical drives and demands made upon the entire personality. These drives can be an influence toward life or death depending upon the state or condition of the believer at the time. The carnal mind always produces death; the spiritual or renewed mind produces life and peace. The drives in themselves are not sinful; the implementation of the drive may or may not be.

In summary, the natural man is "in the flesh" and can do nothing but walk "in the flesh". The carnal or fleshly man is "in the Spirit" but walks "after the flesh." The spiritual man is "in the Spirit" and walks "in the Spirit" or "after the Spirit."

Now, to return to the former method of portraying the interactions within the individual, Diagram 11 depicts a person who has chosen by a definite act of volition and faith to choose or reckon upon his position and resources in Christ

A DAILY AND
CONTINUOUS
PROCESS
(LUKE 9:23 AND
2 COR. 4:11)

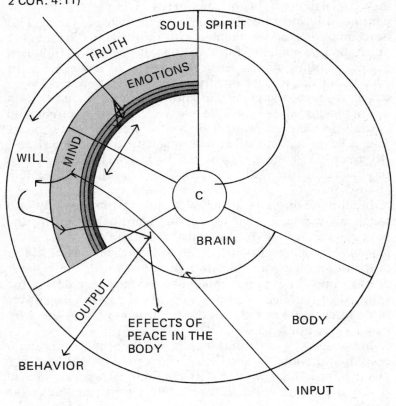

*DIAGRAM 11*

152

with the resultant change in behavior. By denying self (Luke 9:23) or choosing against himself he yields his members as "instruments of righteousness unto God" rather than yielding his "members as instruments of unrighteousness unto sin" (Romans 6:13).

Since the behavior is instigated by the content or program in the mind at the behest of the will, the logical way to change unprofitable or illogical behavior is to change the program. But, as in any computer center, the accuracy of the program depends upon the skill and dependability of the programmer. If the operator invariably feeds an erroneous program into the computer, the printout or answer will be in error. If the operator only has access to erroneous programs, he has no choice but to produce unacceptable results. This is the plight of the unsaved person; he is under bondage to sin and is programmed by the old man. Not so with the Christian — "For he that is dead is freed from sin" (Romans 6:7). The operator, the will, is no longer bound to sin and erroneous programs but now has the option to choose the Divine Programmer, the Lord Jesus Christ and thereby institute the behavior He deems appropriate — enabling His child to walk in the power of the Spirit!

Once the new program, Truth, is implemented by the volitional choice of the will, the indwelling Christ empowers the believer to behave in accord with truth. John 8:32 states, "And ye shall know the truth and the truth shall make you free." The converse of this statement would be, "And you shall know lies and the lies will enslave you." This is the plight of the neurotic individual; the mind accepts as factual the lies embodied in the emotions and concocted by the flesh or self and the brain implements the lies into behavior.

When instead, truth is volitionally accepted even though it is in contradiction to the emotions, the emotions will respond either gradually or suddenly to the truth. To illustrate this, a lady came for counseling who a month before had been petrified at the thought of the second coming of Christ. However, shortly before the interview she had accepted Christ and was now eagerly anticipating His coming. The truth accepted in her mind had freed her of fear in her emotions.

Diagram 11 shows a great change in the mind as the Lord Jesus Christ does the reprogramming, with a corresponding change in the emotions as the truth is assimilated. As Christ lives through the individual, old emotional and mental patterns give way as the mind or attitudes of Christ (Philippians 2:5) take hold in the life. Even though the initial appropriation of Christ as life takes place as a discrete event (an act of faith) it must be a daily (Luke 9:23) and continuous (2 Corinthians 4:11) action. As we continually yield our wills to His, He continues to deliver the self-life to the cross and manifest or show forth His life through us. Physiological effects, such as headaches, ulcers, hypertension and fatigue, are often reversed as self is dethroned and Christ is enthroned.

## THE PATH TO THE CROSS

As the serious-minded person enters counseling or the Holy Spirit utilizes circumstances and the Word to deal with the flesh, there is a definite process that takes place. In this process there are several identifiable milestones. Sometimes these are not discernible as discrete events, and two or more may occur simultaneously. In this chapter diagrams are used to illustrate some of the typical patterns a person may encounter. While each person has his own unique pattern, the typical descriptions will serve to illustrate the mood swings and variance in personality strength relative to the significant milestones.

### PATTERN #1

The first pattern depicts the individual who comes to

counseling never having had any real victory in his Christian experience. The line indicates his soul strength prior to his conversion. For a period of time, the person's soul strength stays the same or gradually declines as he comes under the convicting power of the Holy Spirit. Then he comes to the point, as indicated by the first event, where he accepts the Lord Jesus Christ as personal Savior. With some this event is very climactic and there are positive changes in the life. This is illustrated by the rise in the line as the Holy Spirit takes control of certain aspects of the life resulting in release from some of the sin that has been in control. This person enjoys a measure of relief for a while and then, generally speaking, his new zeal begins to wear off and he settles down. If he isn't followed up by proper counseling and direction in the Word, he may go down even lower than before. Spiritual counsel can help telescope this into a shorter period of time. As he goes along, he finds that he is unable to live the Christian life. There is no victory in his life, nor is he being used of the Lord.

When he realizes the Christian life just isn't working for him and he has exhausted his alternatives, he comes up to the place of complete surrender or total commitment. There are many patterns after complete surrender, but usually there is some improvement since he has quit fighting God and enjoys a measure of peace. Then as time goes on, things get worse. Many times he questions the validity of his surrender and sometimes even the reality of his salvation.

The arrows are indicative of the fact that a person may try many things to make self stronger and prevent coming to the end of himself. Among these are rationalization, compulsive church work, tranquilizers, psychotherapy, etc. With the passing of time he may study the Word and profit from the help of a friend or counseling through which the Holy Spirit makes him aware of another truth — he must appropriate his identification with Christ in death, burial, resurrection, ascension, and being seated in heavenly places. As his defeat

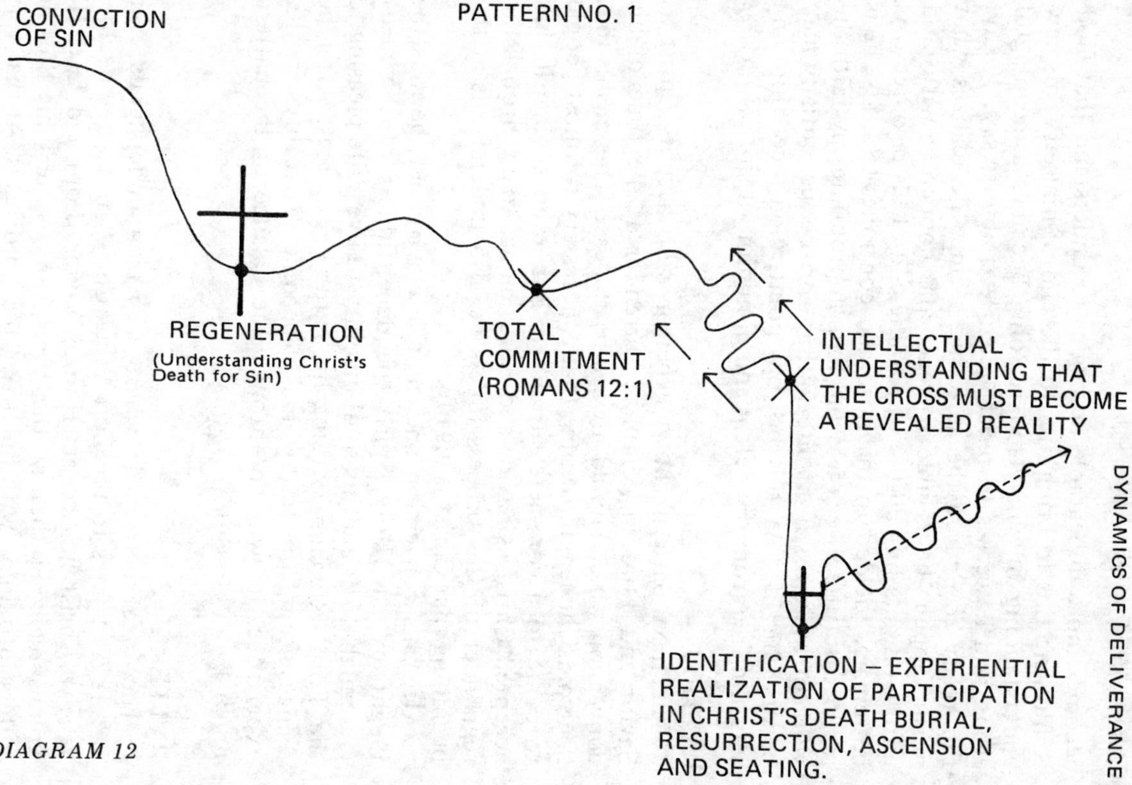

PATTERN NO. 1

CONVICTION
OF SIN

REGENERATION
(Understanding Christ's
Death for Sin)

TOTAL
COMMITMENT
(ROMANS 12:1)

INTELLECTUAL
UNDERSTANDING THAT
THE CROSS MUST BECOME
A REVEALED REALITY

IDENTIFICATION — EXPERIENTIAL
REALIZATION OF PARTICIPATION
IN CHRIST'S DEATH BURIAL,
RESURRECTION, ASCENSION
AND SEATING.

*DIAGRAM 12*

157

becomes more unbearable he begins to understand that God is allowing this to bring him to the end of himself. This new understanding of what God is doing becomes a meaningful event, and he ceases to resist God. He is able to say, "Okay, I'm ready to endure the suffering." Since he realizes what must happen, he is able to relax and cooperate with God until God gets him all the way to the end of his resources. As he remains yielded to the Lord and continues to study, he is reduced to utter weakness and then appropriates by faith the work of the cross in his life so that Christ experientially may become his life. At this bottom point, God meets him and sets him free from the defeat and dominion of sin.

## PATTERN #2

The next pattern shows a person who accepts Christ as Savior and Lord in complete surrender at the time of his conversion which should always be the case. This means that he avoids the length of time that is necessary for most people to come to a complete surrender. But, even though he has accepted Christ as Savior and Lord, he has to go through the remainder of this process unless he also understands at the beginning that Christ is his life.

After his conversion and complete surrender, he must be taught by the Holy Spirit the deceitfulness of the heart (Jeremiah 17:9)and his total inability to live a life pleasing to the Lord (Romans 7) using his natural resources. After he realizes that the cross must become a reality in his experience, he will go through the balance of the pattern much as in pattern #1.

## PATTERN #3

The ideal pattern is where a person understands even before he comes to the Lord Jesus Christ that when he does receive Christ he accepts Him as Savior, Lord and Life. He comes realizing that at the time Christ enters his life, he enters into union with the life of the Lord Jesus. At that very

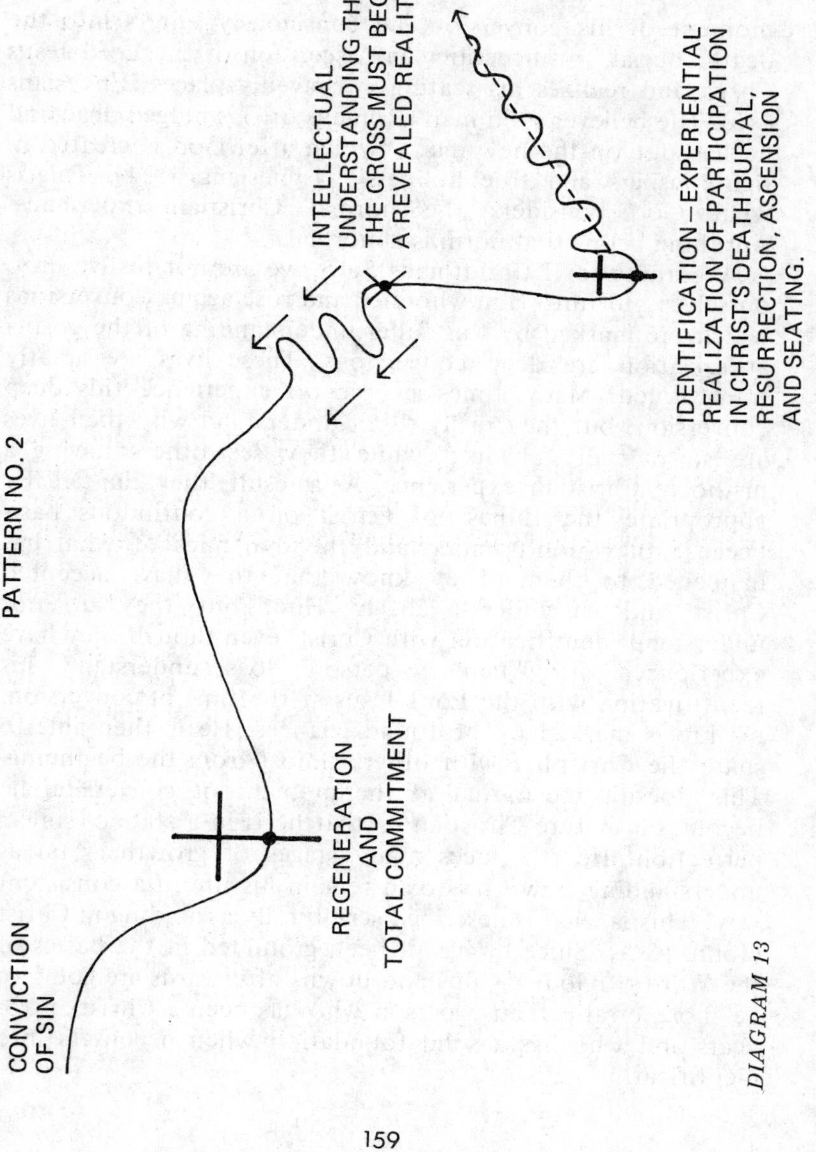

DYNAMICS OF DELIVERANCE

PATTERN NO. 2

CONVICTION OF SIN

REGENERATION AND TOTAL COMMITMENT

INTELLECTUAL UNDERSTANDING THAT THE CROSS MUST BECOME A REVEALED REALITY

IDENTIFICATION—EXPERIENTIAL REALIZATION OF PARTICIPATION IN CHRIST'S DEATH BURIAL, RESURRECTION, ASCENSION AND SEATING.

*DIAGRAM 13*

moment of his conversion, he consciously enters into the death, burial, resurrection and ascension of the Lord Jesus Christ and realizes his seating in heavenly places (Ephesians 2:6). The believer's old man (Romans 6:6) is judged dead and he has put on the new man, "which after God is created in righteousness and true holiness" (Ephesians 4:24). This is what God considers the normal Christian experience. Anything below that norm is abnormal.

According to II Corinthians 5:15, we are not to live unto ourselves but unto Him who died and rose again. Conversions which are marked by this fuller understanding of the gospel at salvation are deep conversions. These lives are greatly transformed. Many times people do experience this deep conversion, but they really don't understand why their lives are so radically changed while they see others having a mediocre Christian experience. As a result, they can't really appropriate the fulness of Christ on a continuous basis because they don't understand the dynamics of what has happened to them. They know that they have accepted Christ and surrendered all to Him, but they do not understand identification with Christ, even though they have experienced it. When a person does understand his identification with the Lord Jesus at the time of conversion, his life is marked by profound changes. He is then able to share the Christ-life with others almost from the beginning. This doesn't mean that at the moment of conversion he becomes a mature Christian or that he is in a state of sinless perfection. He still faces many stages of growth as far as understanding how Christ can remain his life in a consistent way. This is what is described scripturally as abiding in Christ (John 15:5). Since he hasn't been grounded in the basics of the Word of God, his ups and downs afterwards are going to be more erratic than a person who has been a Christian for years and who has a solid foundation when he enters into identification.

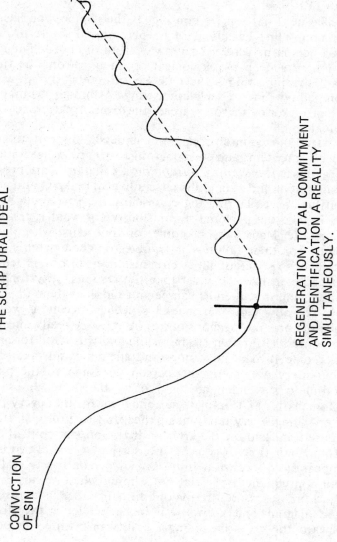

PATTERN NO. 3

THE SCRIPTURAL IDEAL

CONVICTION
OF SIN

REGENERATION, TOTAL COMMITMENT
AND IDENTIFICATION A REALITY
SIMULTANEOUSLY.

*DIAGRAM 14*

161

## PATTERN #4

The next pattern we consider is the person who has come for counseling because he has encountered severe problems. This person may have been away from the Lord, living in sin and having deep psychological problems. From the time of his salvation things have gone progressively downward compelling him to seek counseling. Although he may have minor victories in some areas, the overall pattern is one of defeat.

After the counselor gains an understanding of the counselee's problem and personal history, the wheel and line diagrams in *Handbook To Happiness,* Chapter 2, are presented to help him understand his psychological makeup and also his spiritual need. During the counseling the first thing he must do is take the personal responsibility for what is transpiring in his life. Many persons come for counseling who place the blame for their failures or troubles on their parents, mates, their jobs or lack of jobs, circumstances, or others generally. After he realizes he must take the responsibility for his life and his failures, then he can begin to look at them objectively and see how God can meet his need. Once he is willing to face his personal responsibility, he must be ready and willing to confess all known sin in his life and trust God for grace to overcome it. The next step (and all this could take place in one interview) is for the person to come to the place of complete surrender of his life to the Lord Jesus Christ (Romans 12:1). Complete surrender means that every person, every thing, every relationship, health, the future, all rights to himself are laid on the altar so that God can control the life from that time forward. The surrender is never made to appear easy because it isn't easy. A person has to realize the full consequences of what he is doing when he surrenders to the Lord Jesus. Before making his surrender, he has seen the line diagram and knows that his surrender is the first step toward the cross becoming a reality in his life (his personal

Gethsemane). He knows that he is giving his permission for God to do the work in His way and His time. At this juncture, there are two or three patterns which may typify God's dealing in his life.

## PATTERN #4a

If a person at this point of complete surrender is all the way to the end of himself and the Holy Spirit reveals to him the corruptness of self or the flesh, he is ready to claim by faith his identification with Christ. He has been fighting it all the way and he finally lets go in complete surrender and God meets him and revolutionizes his life. God accepts the surrender, reveals the indwelling Christ, and the person is set free. When a person is at the bottom he can't go any lower and God reaches him there. This scene is repeated many times in counseling since a significant percentage of those who find themselves in the counseling office are there as a last resort.

## PATTERN #4b

There are those who can surrender without reservation or mental equivocation to Christ as Lord and definitely want all that God has for them; yet, they have not been convinced or convicted of the utter rottenness of the flesh and their total inability to live a life pleasing to God. For a person such as this to pray a prayer and claim Christ as his life would be identical to asking an unsaved person who believes in God but is not convicted of his condition as a sinner to pray and receive Christ. Neither prayer would be meaningful since each person is attempting to appropriate beyond the light given him by the Holy Spirit. For some, a more honest prayer is, "I'm not willing, God; but I'm willing for you to make me willing." Or, "I do not have the faith to lay hold of your promises so, right now, I trust you to give me that faith."

A person whose feelings or emotions are at variance with

the facts finds it doubly hard to believe that God will honor His Word and release him from defeat, despair, depression, etc. Even though he sees the true picture of the flesh or self and claims by faith his victory in Christ through the operation of the cross in his life, it may be some time before he begins to sense a release from the symptoms (mental, emotional, etc.) to which he has been enslaved. However, in response to his prayer of faith the Holy Spirit is faithful to apply the work of the cross that the freedom of identification with Christ may become a revealed reality in the believer's life.

This pattern amounts to maintaining a faith position, standing on God's promise of victory until that victory is manifested to God's glory. The victory may come in areas of the life which are completely insignificant to outsiders but very real to the one who has been enslaved to the power of sin and the flesh. There may be a succession of such small victories or there may be a major breakthrough as the Spirit of God faithfully performs His work of controlling or filling (Ephesians 5:18) and thereby mortifies "the deeds of the body" (Romans 8:13).

## PATTERN #5

There are those who have in the past accepted the Lord, surrendered to Him, and have been in full-time service or very active in lay work for a period of years. Now their spiritual service and/or their families are beginning to fall apart. They are in a very definite pattern of self-condemnation and feel like total failures. They think they have been completely disobedient to the "heavenly vision." They come for counseling to analyze what has happened and determine what is wrong. Two variations are given to illustrate the reactions of persons of this type.

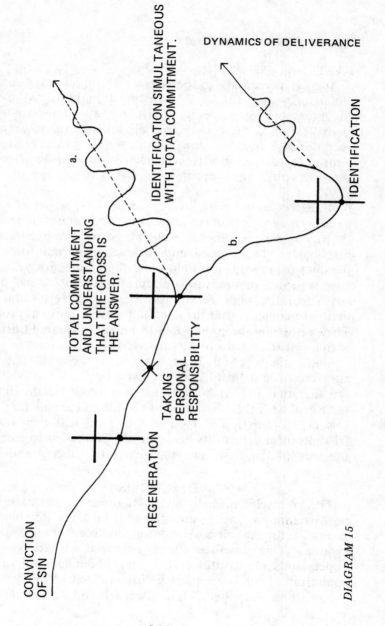

PATTERN NO. 4

DYNAMICS OF DELIVERANCE

CONVICTION OF SIN

REGENERATION

TAKING PERSONAL RESPONSIBILITY

TOTAL COMMITMENT AND UNDERSTANDING THAT THE CROSS IS THE ANSWER.

IDENTIFICATION SIMULTANEOUS WITH TOTAL COMMITMENT.

IDENTIFICATION

a.

b.

*DIAGRAM 15*

165

## PATTERN #5a

A good percentage of persons of this type who come to understand the truths of their position in Christ by the enlightenment of the Holy Spirit, realize immediately that identification is the answer to their spiritual dilemma, and it becomes a reality to them. With others, a release from their symptoms follows shortly after identification with Christ has been accepted and appropriated by faith.

## PATTERN #5b

Other counselees in the same condition cannot believe that theirs could be a spiritual problem. They have been actively involved in the ministry and in reaching others for Christ, possibly on the mission field or in the pulpit. For years they have regarded themselves as mature Christians. Other people have held the same regard for them. As a result, they are loathe to consider that they actually have a spiritual problem. They refuse to accept the fact that they are carnal Christians — that self still controls the life.

Many times there is resistance to the point of open antagonism and hostility as a person begins to struggle with the fact that indeed he is not a mature Christian. He must then deal with this hostility and be able to see and admit that this is his situation as God sees it. God will even use this frustration and hostility to bring the counselee to surrender the way of the flesh and experience the liberty and life in Christ.

## DIAGNOSIS

The counselor must be aware of these various patterns of positive and negative growth and be able to help the counselee to take spiritual inventory and see where he is in the process. This involves first, exploring what a person understands of salvation. Next, his understanding of total commitment or surrender is investigated. Finally, he is probed regarding his (1) intellectual and (2) experiential

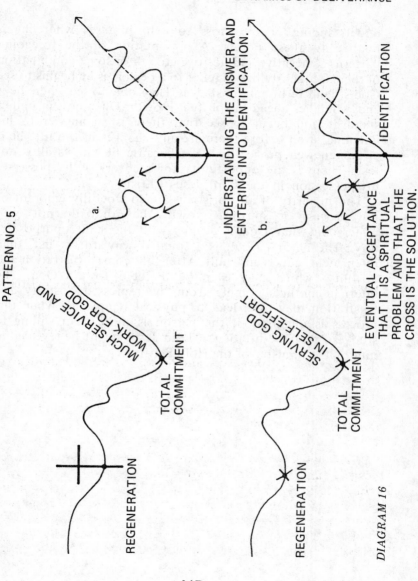

PATTERN NO. 5

REGENERATION

TOTAL COMMITMENT

MUCH SERVICE AND WORK FOR GOD

a.

UNDERSTANDING THE ANSWER AND ENTERING INTO IDENTIFICATION.

IDENTIFICATION

REGENERATION

TOTAL COMMITMENT

SERVING GOD IN SELF-EFFORT

b.

EVENTUAL ACCEPTANCE THAT IT IS A SPIRITUAL PROBLEM AND THAT THE CROSS IS THE SOLUTION.

IDENTIFICATION

DIAGRAM 16

167

understanding of the cross to help him see where he is relative to these points. A presentation of the foregoing patterns of negative and positive growth or some combination of them frequently brings relief to a person as he begins to see God's hand in his circumstances. He is able to see where he is and what lies ahead in spiritual growth. Once he can understand it and begin to see that there is an answer to his dilemma, even before there are any changes in the life, he is given renewed peace and hope because he knows all is not lost. There is the opportunity for recovery as he possesses his possession in the Lord Jesus Christ.

The majority of all Christians are so woefully ignorant of the process of spiritual growth that they do not even understand that God is dealing with them in a purposeful way. The natural result is a spiral downward at first, then resentment, anger, and guilt. After that comes frustration and hostility, which may even be directed toward God. The internal conflicts coming from the repressed hostility and frustration may even lead to physical symptoms. When this process is understood, the person is more than willing to study so that the life of the Lord Jesus might be revealed in him by the ministry of the Holy Spirit.

## SUMMARY

At the beginning of the counseling process, the counselor is to help the person understand himself both psychologically and spirtually. Once the psychological understanding is attained, *there is no further work done so far as trying to change the psychological symptoms or behavior patterns.* In other words, do not stoop to therapy when God has called you to ministry! Then, the spiritual assessment is made, and the person is led to understand the next stage in his spiritual development. If the person is unsaved, he is challenged at this point to receive the Lord Jesus Christ in an unconditional surrender. If he has already accepted Christ, the next step is to see if he knows Jesus Christ as Lord. If he does not, he is challenged to pray in the interview and to surrender all to the Lord Jesus Christ.

If he has accepted Christ both as Savior and Lord, he is helped to understand the process of being brought to the end of himself, since his total surrender was his permission for God to begin this process. After the person understands that this is God's method of deliverance, he is challenged to claim by faith his death, burial, resurrection and ascension with Christ *if* he has been convicted and prepared by the Holy Spirit to do so. If not, he is challenged to surrender or claim that which he honestly can and yield to the working of the Holy Spirit to complete the work in his life.

It is the counselor's task in this and succeeding interviews to go to the bottom with the person as he goes through the downward spiral to the end of self's domination. The counselor explains the Word, the suffering, and the trials that coming to the end of self entails.

He does not remain detached and uninvolved because Christ shows His compassion through the counselor. So as the counselor is willing to continue in the fellowship of Christ's sufferings (Philippians 3:10), he is poured out like a drink offering (Philippians 2:17). The counselor becomes open,

169

transparent and vulnerable as Christ's love is poured out through the counselor to the counselee.

Again we see that the Holy Spirit uses a principle which is the opposite of the psychotherapist's detachment. Even some schools of theology teach their students not to become too involved in counseling and maintain their "professional relationship" with the counselee.

While the counselor has empathy he is not to try compulsively to help the other person with his problems, since this can provide a source of strength to the self life which is in the process of being weakened.

Only God can reveal these truths to those He is using as counselors. Natural human wisdom fails completely to understand as all Spirituotherapy counselors will attest from the times they have tried to coast on their own intellect and counseling abilities.

## VICTORY IN THE VICTOR
Sin was our master —
We, its willing slave; (Rom. 6:20)
The "old man" triumphant
Twixt birth and the grave.
Its death knell sounded
As the veil was rent;
Christ died on the cross, (Rom. 5:8)
And sin's fury was spent.

When He rose from the dead
Victorious o'er sin,
He offered new life (John 5:24)
To those of our kin.
He ascended to Heaven (Acts 1:9)
To the Father's right hand; (Heb. 12:2)
There to seat us in glory (Eph. 2:6)
Sin's presence to remand.

In Christ we died to sin; (Rom. 6:11)
But sin — it did not die
And through our personalities
For control it still does vie.
When by permission or deceit
Our wills it does enmesh (Rom. 6:13a)
We have given reign
To an enemy called Flesh.

Though the "old man" died with Christ (Rom. 6:6)
The flesh (self) is with us still; (Gal. 5:17)
We accede to it's behest
In the domain of our will. (Rom. 6:12)
The flesh, too, is crucified
With its affections and lusts (Gal. 5:24)
To bring its deeds to death (Rom. 8:13)
The cross again we trust! (II Cor. 4:11)

Now, with our Head in the Heavenlies (Eph. 2:6)
And our feet on the Earth
Our minds are renewed (Rom. 12:2)
To know our true worth. (Eph. 1:6)
Our talk is affected
By Christ our true Head;
Our walk is affected (Gal. 5:25)
As by Him we are led. (Rom. 8:14)

Constant victory is promised (II Cor. 2:14)
As in Christ we are placed; (I Cor. 1:30)
It becomes our portion
As self (flesh) is effaced. (Gal. 5:24)
As He lives His life (Gal. 2:20b)
Which only is meet,
His joy in us — our joy is full (John 15:11)
In Him we are complete! (Col. 2:9,10)

# THE INS AND OUT OF REJECTION

# Dynamics of Death/ Resurrection

CHAPTER

7

The purpose of this chapter is to delineate some of the typical psychological and spiritual phenomena that a person endures as he comes to the end of his own resources and experiences the cross. At the outset it should be stressed that "experiences," as such, should not be emphasized. A person should not be oriented during the counseling process or during the study of the Word to believe that he must have a particular experience, or even some discernible event that takes place that assures him he has come to the point of identification. However, there must be that enlightening of a person by the Holy Spirit of the reality of his participation in the death, burial, resurrection and ascension of the Lord Jesus; His Spirit witnesses with our spirit (Romans 8:16).

This may or may not be discernible at a point in time. Recognition of how it happened isn't necessary, but there must be the freedom from within, the reality that it is the Christ life, however it comes about in the individual's experience. It sounds like a contradiction in terms to say this must be true in our experience, and yet we are not to look for an experience. There must be something that happens within this person which frees him from the old power and changes his life from past patterns. This may take place in an identifiable crisis or it may not. Much depends upon the personality of the individual. Some persons are geared toward a climactic type of thing, while others are psychologically likely to be dealt with in a more gradual manner. The Holy Spirit deals with each person in a way he understands. If it is a gradual identification awareness it won't present him with any real threat, but the counselee should be prepared for an emotional crisis in case this is the way in which God deals with him.

A person, during a crisis of this type, could have some difficulty discerning what is real and what isn't. It could also be an emotional release where tears or laughter are involved, or a person may have an acute sense of total freedom. However, for the person who has been neurotic or psychotic much of his life, freedom can be a very frightening thing. Just the prospect of freedom may prevent a person from letting go because he can't say, in truth, that he really wants to be completely healed and set free. Since he has never experienced freedom, he may have real fear of the responsibility which freedom enjoins. Actually, he does not become free and responsible to do it all himself, but rather free to let Christ carry his burden and to live His life within him.

We have described the culmination or termination of the identification process. Yet it is really a beginning because as soon as a person has entered into identification, he begins another process of learning to live a life of daily reckoning upon His one-time crucifixion with Christ (Luke 9:23).

As he reaches this beginning point, there are many things that the counselee doesn't understand. It becomes the responsibility of the counselor, the spiritual guide, to interpret some of these emotions, events or disturbances to the individual as he goes through them so that he understands the process and doesn't remain in a state of confusion, and possibly panic. It is very comforting to the individual to have explained to him, as he is going through trials and depressions, that these events are not at all unusual. He is coming to an end and a beginning as others have, and this is all part of healthy spiritual growth — negative and positive.

Starting with the person who has been saved in the counseling interview, it is necessary to get him into Bible study and get him situated in a Bible-believing church where he is given the opportunity for fellowship with other believers. Initially, there may be a spurt of freedom and, depending upon the individual, this may continue to develop so that the freedom from bondage to the flesh through identification with the Lord is real from the beginning. In such cases the individual may just blossom like a flower and seemingly require very little cultivation. As he understands his position in Christ, he appropriates Christ's resources and lives on a high plane. This is a very healthy birth and growth and is, of course, the ideal situation. However, a baby Christian usually requires much care as he studies the Word and exercises his spiritual muscles. Much fellowship outside the counseling interview, preferably in the context of the local church, is very desirable.

The person who makes a total surrender in the interview and experiences freedom and identification at the same time is in need of spiritual nurture and growth, but it doesn't take as much work in counseling with this person as it does with a person who makes a total commitment but does not enter into the reality of identification immediately. This person is the focus of much turmoil because the total commitment is merely the person's permission for God to begin to work in his life to bring him to the end of his resources and resolve the psychological conflict.

He may begin to experience some sense of relief and freedom as he surrenders because he has ceased fighting God. As the Holy Spirit begins to work within him and just before he comes to the place where he experientially gives up control of his life, a person usually feels a sensation of frustration, anxiety, and depression. It is at these times that the counselor must be able to reassure the person that this is not an unusual occurrence. This depression, anxiety and insecurity may cause a person to question his salvation or have some suicidal thoughts. He is usually going through a period where he questions God. He can't see why this kind of a process should be necessary and why he should have to endure all this suffering. To him it seems unfair that other Christians just seem to sail through life and have no problems, and yet here he is serving the Lord, completely surrendered, and he has to go through all this!

Many times this person vents his hostility on God. In fact, in counseling he is encouraged to tell God that he is really upset with Him. God knows it anyway, so he might as well verbalize it and admit it to himself. Also, it should be understood that this suffering isn't always a steady downward process. There are many times when it levels off and a person senses nothing happening, either good or bad. Then he is upset by that because he thinks he should be making progress and possibly God has forgotten about his case.

Sometimes there is such improvement in a person's psychological adjustment or happiness that he may think that he must have appropriated Christ as life because the downward process eases off for awhile. After a while he finds that it wasn't a spiritual reality but an intellectual and emotional release; he must still be further reduced in weakness. Many times it is impossible for the counselor to know definitely whether the counselee has appropriated Christ as life or not. It is better for the counselor not to verbalize any spiritual assessments but to encourage the counselee to take a faith position and expect God to make the necessary transformation in His time. Self dies hard and will even fake death to keep from really relinquishing control.

## At the End of Self

What does it mean to come to the end of self or to the end of our resources? This question can't be answered in any stereotyped way as far as recognizing it in each individual. It takes place differently in each life. It really depends on the person's psychological makeup and the strength of his will. There are, however, some typical patterns which are worthy of consideration.

## The Intellectual Pattern

A person who has been steeped in intellectual pursuit through formal education or in his own study often finds it extremely difficult to permit God to work in his life in a way that is illogical to him. He has so long relied upon his intellectual ability that he attempts to fathom the deep things of God through human wisdom. A thorough knowledge of psychology, philsophy and even theology can be a decided hindrance when it does not square with the revealed truth of God's Word. First Corinthians 1:27 states, "But God hath chosen the foolish things of the world to confound the wise; and God hath chosen the weak things of the world to confound the things which are mighty." In I Corinthians 2:14 Paul emphasizes, "But the natural man receiveth not the things of the Spirit of God: for they are foolishness unto him: neither can he know them, because they are spiritually discerned." Christians also make the mistake of trying to reason with their minds and act upon the dictates of the Scriptures in the strength of their minds and wills rather than relying upon the communion of God through their spirits.

Some theologians are prime examples of persons whose

technical understanding of the Scriptures may hinder the Holy Spirit from applying the truth to their hearts through spiritual and practical illumination. The simplicity of resting in their position in Christ overwhelms and confounds them. Some intellectuals must personally try all of the blind alleys and come to the place of seeming intellectual suicide before they are willing to accept the simplicity of merely taking God at His word. When their mental and emotional resources are bankrupted, they have no choice but to turn in childlike faith to the spiritual.

Knowingly or unknowingly, their pursuits have been for truth, and God's Word promises that "ye shall know the truth, and the truth shall make you free" (John 8:32). They must finally realize that truth is not a philosophy or an intellectual pursuit, but truth is embodied in the person of Jesus Christ. "I am the way, the *truth,* and the life" (John 14:6).

They have come to the end intellectually and find the fullness of Christ there; then they find it is the most rational, intellectual understanding possible – just to take God at His word and simply rest in it. The Apostle Paul must have travelled this way in his quest for victory.

## The Emotional Pattern

Probably the majority of believers do not have serious intellectual hang-ups concerning God's Word and His dealing with them. They may be well-adjusted psychologically and getting along pretty well in life. When God begins to deal with them and they begin to find life empty, they realize there is an unsatisfied need with which they must deal – or a person may have been neurotic since childhood and begins to crumble under the responsibilities of life.

Mild or severe anxiety begins to take its toll and an answer must be found. Frequently, a person goes outside the church and away from God to find answers and only discovers increasing frustration and guilt. When the anxiety is no longer bearable or its negative effect on the spouse and/or family disrupts normal living, the person is willing to seek God's answer for his life.

In God's dealing with the individual it is not only expected but desirable that depletion of emotional reserves or resources be accomplished. It is only as the soul strength is broken that God can begin to meet a person's real needs. As the person becomes increasingly unable to cope with life, he has no choice but to let go of self and let God bring about His perfect will in his life. The depression and anxiety can be almost too much to handle for a person who has never experienced it; he may think the world is coming to an end. For the neurotic person it is a way of life; it is merely increased in its intensity. A person who has had a neurotic break may fear that another is in the making and try to hold on for dear life to avoid it. Of course, he is holding on to *self* when he does this.

It is always an awesome and somewhat frightening prospect to lose control, which is exactly what must happen if God is to take control. As the Holy Spirit makes the life of Christ a reality within the individual, his life is integrated psychologically, spiritually and physically.

The impulsive Apostle Peter followed his emotions while with the Lord and while "walking afar off" until he began to be led by the Spirit after the resurrection.

**The Physical Pattern**

Sometimes illness in the body is utilized by God to weaken a person to the point where he will turn to God and seek a more meaningful relationship.

In other cases, psychological conflict is so great that a person's physical strength is depleted to the point that he can no longer function adequately. There have been actual cases in the history of Spirituotherapy where Christians were reduced in strength as to be almost nonfunctional, and God met them in this extremity.

Job was permitted of the Lord to suffer in the body that he might come to the place where his sole dependence was upon God for his very existence.

## SUMMARY

The coming to the end of soul-strength is usually a combination of intellectual, emotional and physical components. Without the knowledge of the process which is taking place, it can be a very frightening phenomenon. When many persons are just at the point where God can work in their lives, they turn to non-spiritual therapy to build back what God has permitted to be torn down, thus subverting the process and prolonging the agony.

As the person reaches the extremity of his resources and yields to the sovereign work of the Holy Spirit, he experiences a freedom and peace previously unknown to him. This may occur as he reads some portion of God's Word, or hears a message in word or in song. There have been those with whom God deals in their sleep in order to bypass their conscious thought processes.

It may be a gradual dawning or a crisis revelation. One lady wept all day long and didn't know the reason until she experienced freedom and release as the result. Each comes to the place where he can no longer go on in his own way and God meets him in a unique manner such that he knows it is of God, not of men, especially not the counselor.

It is certain that if we remain yielded to God's working in our lives that He will meet and free us from our self-bondage. Romans 5:10 states, "For if, when we were enemies, we were reconciled to God by the death of His Son, much more, being reconciled, we shall be saved [from self] by his life" — both here and hereafter.

The counselor's task is to go through this downward process with the individual. During this time the counselor will hear many complaints, some hostility, and much despair as the person comes to the end. He must go with the person through the heartaches and trials if he is to share in the joy as the person is set free.

The process is much akin to that of a midwife during the

birth process. When the crisis is traumatic in nature it is very reassuring to have the counselor there to pray with the person and read from the Scripture as self goes through the death throes. Even though the person may understand to some extent and be desirous for God to complete the work, there is the involuntary resistance as the transition from the self-life to the Christ-life takes place.

However, it is not just a death process; it is also a resurrection life process. It is not the "new birth" but it is in a sense a metamorphosis where Christ begins to live His life through the individual. The counselee goes through the death process, the life process and will experience the regressions to self-control afterwards which are described in Chapter 9.

# Dynamics of Discipline

# 8

## WALKING IN THE SPIRIT

In the process of deliverance from enslaving attitudes and behaviors, there is usually the initial freedom, either gradually or through the Holy Spirit, dealing with the person in a crisis. This may or may not be accompanied by a confirmation in the emotions initially. Just as in conversion, some are affected immediately in the emotions; others are not. Since it is a step of faith in God's promises through the exercising of the will, it is not necessary that the emotions be touched for a definite spiritual transaction to take place.

Likewise, there are those with whom God deals in a sovereign manner whose lives are transformed but who do not intellectually understand what has happened. This was true of John Stevens, the chairman of the board of directors of Grace Fellowship International. His life reflected a walk in the Spirit which was wonderful for him, but he was unable to share it with anyone else. He had led many to Christ but could not lead them to enjoy the victory he knew, since he could not articulate it. Once he understood intellectually or mentally, he could then communicate the Christ-life to others.

This has been true of many. Some could not sustain the victory God had given because they did not understand operationally what God had done. Thus, they did not know how to cooperate with Him in retaining the victory He had given.

In the previous chapter it was illustrated that the death-resurrection process freed one from the negative attitudes and behaviors or the power of sin. The initial freedom or entering into the spiritual Canaan is a break with the old life, but there is much ground to be reclaimed and much new ground to be taken. There may be instantaneous deliverance from some defeating attitudes and behavior while others are not even touched or brought to conscious awareness. This is parallel to sins in a person's life at conversion. Some drop away immediately while others are pointed out by the Holy Spirit at a later stage in the growth process.

To illustrate the walk in the Spirit, the wheel diagram is again employed to indicate separate functions within the spirit of man. (Diagram 17).

A glance at the diagram will show that just as man is a trinity of spirit, soul and body, so also are the three aspects of man divided into three components. The three components of the soul — mind, will and emotions — can be understood by the diagrams and discussion in Chapter 4, Part 2. The three components of the physical body — flesh, bones and blood — are self-evident but this is not so with the spirit of man. However, rather than present a lengthy case in defense of intuition, conscience and communion, let me refer the reader to Chapter 5 of *What Is Man?* by T. Austin-Sparks (Ministry of Life Inc.). Other well-known writers such as Ruth Paxson and Watchman Nee are agreed on this threefold makeup of the spirit of man.

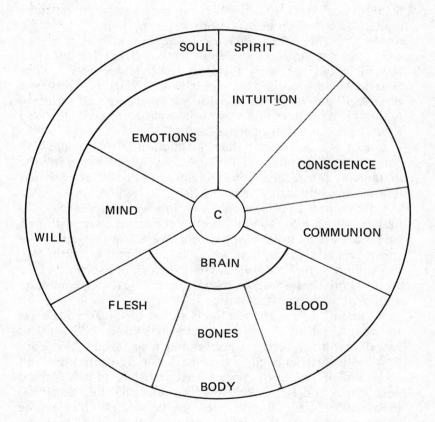

*DIAGRAM 17*

*Intuition* is the organ of spiritual intelligence by which we may know things which we have never learned through our minds. Also, through our intuition God can give us direct leading as regards His will for our lives though it must be confirmed by other means before we act upon it.

Through our *communion* or fellowship with Him in our spirit, we are able to abide in the love that He has shed abroad in our hearts by the Holy Spirit (Romans 5:5). The function of intuition in the spirit would roughly correspond to that of intelligence in the soul. We might say that intuition is our "receiver" whereby we are sensitive to God's leading apart from the senses or sense data.

*Conscience* would correlate in function to that of the will. We may choose volitionally to act in accordance with the dictates of conscience or to violate it; to do the latter would be to knowingly walk "after the flesh."

Communion and emotions have somewhat in common. We may relate to others in an emotional manner demonstrating such qualities as love, hostility, etc. We relate to God in the spirit; worship or communion is in spirit and in truth. We can't *think* or *feel* our way to God; He is in our spirits and we are in Him. Therefore, we relate, communicate, or commune with God in our spiritual nature.

Diagram 18 depicts the effects stated in the Word relative to the integration of spirit, soul and body of the believer who is walking in the Spirit. A person may hear through the Word that he has participated in the death, burial, resurrection and ascension of the Lord Jesus Christ and that he is identified with Christ and His cross. However, until the Holy Spirit has prepared or drawn him, it is mere intellectual assent. When he is drawn by the Holy Spirt and responds through his will by an act of faith, the Holy Spirit performs the work of renewing his mind as promised in Romans 12:2. The intellectual belief of the truth must be accompanied by the revelation or illumination of the Holy Spirit. Paul put it this way in

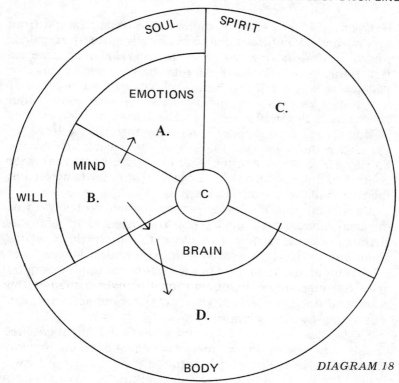

DIAGRAM 18

A. Phil. 4:6a Do not be anxious about anything. (NIV)
Phil. 4:7 And the peace of God . . . will guard your hearts and your minds in Christ Jesus. (NIV)

B. Rom. 12:2 ". . . Be transformed by the renewing of your mind."
Luke 24:45 — "He opened their minds so they could understand the scriptures." (NIV)
Titus 3:5 . . . Renewal by the Holy Spirit. (NIV)
Eph. 4:22,23 . . . Put off your old self . . . to be made new in the attitude of your minds. (NIV)
Rom. 8:6 . . . The mind controlled by the Spirit is Life and Peace. (NIV)
Eph. 1:18, 19 I pray also that the eyes of your heart may be enlightened in order that you may know the hope to which he has called you, the riches of his glorious inheritance in the saints, and his incomparably great power for us who believe. (NIV)

C. Eph. 3:16,19 . . . That He may strengthen you with power through His Spirit in your inner being . . . that you may be filled to the measure of all the fullness of God. (NIV)
Col. 2:9, 10      I Cor. 2: 10-14      I Cor. 1:30

D. Rom. 8:11 . . . He who raised up Jesus from the dead will also give life to your mortal bodies through his Spirit, who lives in you. (NIV)
Ps. 42:11 . . . The health of my countenance

Galatians 1:15,16: "It pleased God, who separated me from my mother's womb, and called me by his grace, to reveal his son in me." He *is* in us but He is only *revealed* in us as we are transformed by the renewing of our minds.

Once the Christ-life is a reality and we have a renewed mind, it is necessary to understand the interaction of soul and spirit as the Holy Spirit would direct our walk to keep us in victory and accomplish His ministry through us. If we are to walk in the Spirit (Galatians 5:17) we must be led by the Spirit. To be led by the Spirit we must have a mind controlled by the Spirit. Whatever or whoever controls our minds will likewise control our walk.

As we walk in the Spirit, He may choose to reveal to us through our intuition some action He wishes us to take. Or, He may express His life and love to others through our communion with Him without our express knowledge, either intuitively or intellectually. In the former, He impresses upon us intuitively the course of action, and this must be communicated through our spirit to our mind before we can take action by means of our will.

To illustrate this and elaborate on God's dealing in my life, permit me to detail the manner in which God led me to leave my position in industry to inaugurate the ministry of Grace Fellowship International.

I had not consciously vowed to leave my position upon receiving my master's degree which was to be awarded in December 1969. However, in the late fall I began to sense it was almost time to leave. At times I felt like a displaced person as I walked the corridors, even though I had been there more than eighteen years. Since this could be just another faulty product of my emotions which had driven me for years, I knew I couldn't trust it. I prayed about it and asked God for guidance through His Word if this were of Him. The number 40 kept coming up in my reading and I was coming up on age 40 the next March (one month before my

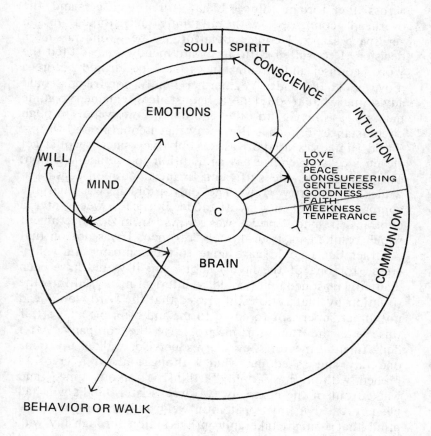

*DIAGRAM 19*

pay terminated with the company, as it turned out). It seemed the Holy Spirit was telling me that my training was completed and that it was now time to begin leading persons across the Jordan. Since I had three teenagers and the overhead connected with a family accustomed to an aerospace salary, I could not afford to be wrong in such a decision. I consulted with my board members since I felt the Word, counsel and circumstances must be aligned before a move could be made. Yet neither family nor friends could advise me what to do. Only circumstances remained to guide me so I prayed to the Lord to intervene through circumstances in such a direct way that I could not go wrong. I told Him I saw a layoff as the only way since I would get eleven weeks severance pay in addition to accrued vacation. This would give me sufficient financial cushion to subsist while the ministry grew. The only problem was that the company was not in a layoff mode. But a few weeks later, a contract stretchout notice was received from the government which resulted in a surplus of 250 men. I was not on that contract but I could have gone to the company and volunteered for one of the layoff spots, and it would have been granted. I reasoned that I could be interjecting myself into the situation by that action so I prayed that the Lord would lead my direct supervisor to come to me and offer me a layoff, if this were the time for me to leave the company. After departmental meetings, etc., my supervisor walked up to me one day and asked me what I thought about a layoff. I replied without hesitation, "I think it's about time," and walked out of the company two weeks later. God's will had been revealed in my spirit intuitively and confirmed in my mind that I might take appropriate action through my will. Despite a lifetime of emotional turmoil, the emotions did not contest this action!

As in God's dealing with me in many other matters, I understood very little of the dynamics at the time, but now some years later it can be written down with empirical evidence to support the conclusion that He was definitely leading in the ensuing developments.

Perhaps the prime function God purposes in and through our spirit is to manifest His love to those in need of spiritual and emotional healing and to be able to "love one another, as He gave us commandment" (I John 3:23). This is one of the results of His overall purpose for our lives which is that we might be conformed to His image (Rom. 8:29). *His love is the all-pervasive antidote to rejection.*

Since such love is not native to our personality and we are commanded to love in this manner, we know He has provided the means through which to channel His love. The previous diagram shows how His love flows through our spirit and soul to others. But what is the Scriptural principle which makes it possible for us to "love one another as I have loved you"? How do we come by such love?

Let's refer to a modification of the line diagram from *Handbook to Happiness,* Chapter 2 (below).

Ephesians 1:3 tells us that He has blessed us in the heavenly realms with every spiritual blessing in Christ, some of which have been graphically presented above. In Ephesians 5:2 we are admonished to live a life of love, just as Christ loved us. Ephesians 3:17-19 states that when we are rooted and established in love we will have the power to grasp the love of Christ and to know this love that we may be filled to the measure of the fullness of God. Philippians 1:9-11 says that our love should abound more and more in knowledge and depth of insight that we may be filled with the fruit of righteousness that comes through Jesus Christ. Colossians 1:5 tells us that faith and love spring from the hope stored up for us in heaven.

Romans 5:5 states that God has poured out His love into our hearts by the Holy Spirit, and I Thessalonians 3:12 calls for our love to increase and *overflow* for each other. Second

Thessalonians 3:5 assures that the Lord will direct our hearts into God's love. First Timothy 1:14 teaches that faith and love are ours in Christ Jesus.

The foregoing should be sufficient warrant for the premise that God's love is appropriated in the same manner as we appropriate His substitutionary work on the cross for salvation. His representative work which provides for our participation in His death, burial, resurrection and ascension are freely bestowed by His sovereign grace! As we are saved by faith (Ephesians 2:8,9) and kept by faith (I Peter 1:5), we can also love by faith! It was His love shown through the cross that won us to Himself. "We love Him, because He first loved us" (I John 4:19). It is the power of His love flowing through us that will secure a hearing for the gospel that others may respond to the ministry of the Spirit and the Word. It is, likewise, His love flowing through us that will mend broken relationships as our rejective behavior is replaced by His selfless love.

As depicted by the arrowheads diagram 19 we must always divest ourselves of selfish motives through the renewed operation of the cross in our lives before we seek to appropriate that spiritual supply in the heavenlies for our spiritual need here on earth. While it is true that we abide in the heavenlies, we nevertheless still live on earth. That is why we must walk here in His power until we are translated into His presence.

But how can we do this? As God patiently hammered this truth home in my own life, I realized that I had not loved my wife in the sense of Ephesians 5:25 and was not naturally equipped to do so (nor is anyone else). As I appropriated by faith His love, she sensed a new quality of love (how, I don't know) and was able to submit to my headship in the spirit of Ephesians 5:22. As the Holy Spirit consummated this relationship we entered into a union in Christ hitherto unknown in twenty-three years of marriage (and three years of

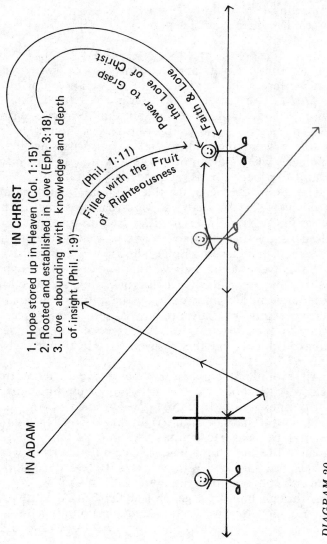

**IN CHRIST**

1. Hope stored up in Heaven (Col. 1:15)
2. Rooted and established in Love (Eph. 3:18)
3. Love abounding with knowledge and depth of insight (Phil. 1:9)

Filled with the Fruit of Righteousness (Phil. 1:11)

Power to Grasp the Love of Christ

Faith & Love

IN ADAM

*DIAGRAM 20*
(See New International Version)

counseling)!

Yes, His grace *is* sufficient!

## TAKE COMMAND!

Our circumstances are frequently so overwhelmingly real that we lose sight (by faith) of *who* we are and *where* we are *in Christ*. Even though the Scripture tells us that we are pilgrims and strangers here and that our citizenship is in Heaven, we are prone to live our lives as though this physical existence were the reality that is of surpassing importance. Similarly, when our emotions tell us that we are inferior we are apt to accept this as fact and act upon it.

The Scripture tells us that we are complete in Christ (Colossians 2:10), that "all spiritual blessings in heavenly places in Christ" (Ephesians 1:3) are ours and that God "hath raised us up together, and made us sit together in heavenly places in Christ Jesus" (Ephesians 2:6). *This* is reality!

We can choose to believe this and live as though it were reality, or we can live as though what we see, feel and experience here (sense data) is the ultimate in reality. Our victory stands or falls on the basis of our choice. Are we going to live our lives on the basis of common sense and things visible or on the basis of faith in things invisible and eternal? Which is reality?

An example from history may serve to illustrate, albeit weakly, our choice to live in terms of circumstances or the reality known only to faith.

General Jonathan Wainwright was second in command to General Douglas McArthur when the Philippines fell to the Japanese during World War II. General McArthur was able to escape but General Wainwright suffered the rigors of the concentration camp at the mercy of his captors.

Although he was a general in the United States Army he had no more authority than did the youngest buck private; all alike were subject to the whim of those who could choose

194

to abuse them or treat them well. The grim reality was that General Wainwright was a Prisoner of War and had no freedom to exercise his privileges as a general in the U.S. Army.

He is now faced with a choice: he can remember his position or he can succumb to the reality as he is currently experiencing it. He can cry the blues and say "I'm nothing, a nobody — the same as every other dogface here." Or, he can maintain his faith position that back in "heavenly places" in the United States he is *still* a general! His incarceration is very real, but back in "heavenly places" his general's pay is going into the bank or to his family because he is very much a general on active duty status.

The acid test comes when one day he gets some sense data via radio and understands that Japan has surrendered! He again has two choices — to bemoan his fate as a nobody or to remember his position as a general. Since he remembered his position, he walked into the office of the commanding officer of the camp and announced that he was taking command! He had fought none of the battles, but he was on the victor's side and shared all of the benefits that the victor had won. His position had never changed, whatever his condition in captivity. His circumstances were real even though temporary; his position was real and unchanging such that without further confirmation he could take command. After two or three years as a prisoner he probably didn't feel like a general, but he remembered who he was and conducted his life accordingly.

We may be surrounded and held captive by circumstances without and by pressures within; nevertheless, we have the sure promise that the victory has been won. We are not only on the Victor's side; we are *in* the Victor, the Lord Jesus Christ in heavenly places and He is in us! We do not have to wait, as did General Wainwright for the victory to be won. Our foe has been vanquished! By faith we may enter into His victory. We can succumb to circumstances (the world), the lie of the enemy without (Satan) and the enemy within (self or flesh); or, we can triumphantly announce in the face of it all, "In Christ I take command" and live our lives to the glory of God from the vantage point of victory.

Our destiny is settled; our position of being complete in Him is secure; we have the privilege of following as He "leads in His triumph in Christ". (II Corinthians 2:14) (NASB)

The triumph in which we share is not only over enemies without but also enemies within. As we choose to abide in Christ we can take charge of our emotions rather than serving them. As we maintain a faith position that Christ is our life and walk in the Spirit we do not fulfill the lust of the flesh. In our emotions, as in other areas of life, we can claim by faith that the truth sets us free. The renewal that takes place in our minds will eventually be reflected in our emotions as well.

# Dealing With Regression and the Adversary

Regression or the return of previous symptoms accompanies reversion to the self-centered or flesh-controlled life. These two topics, regression and the adversary, are considered jointly since self must be in control before Satan has an inside man or accomplice to carry out his dastardly work.

Identification with the Lord Jesus Christ, or the abundant life, is not sinless perfection. The self-life has not been dealt with permanently as has the old man. When we fail to reckon upon our resources in Christ and instead begin again to control our own lives, the flesh and the symptoms connected with it are to be contended with. The symptoms may be in the form of depression, anxiety, frustration, defeat, old obsessions, pride and various forms of mental or emotional symptoms such as neuroses and psychoses. Or, to relate the symptoms to spiritual terminology, the works of the flesh (dead works) are the certain results of the fleshly life.

The counselee should be cautioned, even before he

appropriates his resources in Christ, that he must reckon upon the victory of the cross daily, according to Luke 9:23 and II Corinthians 4:11, in order for the life of Christ daily and continuously to be made manifest in his mortal flesh. Even with that admonition and the subsequent reckoning on the part of the counselee, there is frequently more "down" time than "up" in the early days of the new life. Generally speaking, the first flush of understanding of the new life results in new-found victory, at least for a short period of time. But it isn't too long before the old symptoms reappear and the person begins to think, "Now I've lost it, I'll never have it back, I've goofed up." Self again becomes prominent as he sings the "Woe is Me" blues.

Usually at this time the person calls the counseling office, or a spiritual friend, in deep distress with a need to be informed again of what he is going through and why. He needs to be reassured that he hasn't lost his position in Christ or his stage of growth, but that the flesh is back in control. When the counselor explains this and shows him what the basic problem is, the person can again reckon upon his death to sin and aliveness to God (Romans 6:11) and put his trust completely in the Lord Jesus to lift him from his despair as he again appropriates the cross as a reality in his life. The counselor *is not* to try to deal directly with the depression or other symptoms that have returned, whether they be psychosomatic or psychological. Do not do psychotherapy! Simply show the counselee that he is back under the dominion of sin which creates the condition of self-resurgence.

Very frequently it is during this first down time, this first regression or reversion to self, that Satan manifests himself in an overt way. Satan's usual trick is to ally himself with the person's emotions and/or flesh and start to emphasize and enlarge these out of proportion. For instance, along with the depression that a person may experience, if this has been a symptom of the self-life, Satan will bring on some oppression to amplify the depressive reaction.

Also, during this period of time, negative thoughts run rampant. Satan suggests a few of his own which are in agreement with the way a person is feeling at that time so the automatic tendency for the person is to agree with Satan. His thinking begins a downward spiral as he continues to agree with Satan against God. When Satan can get someone to agree with him against God he has fulfilled his role as "accuser of the brethren" (Revelation 12:10). The role of the counselor is to intervene in this process and help the person to see objectively what is happening and to deal with Satan in a direct manner.

James 4:7 gives us instructions as to what must happen before we begin to deal with Satan: "Submit yourselves therefore to God." When self is in control and we are under satanic attack, *it does little good to rebuke Satan as long as we are still tolerating the reign of sin in our lives.* The first step, therefore, must be to confess any and all known sins and then to submit unto God and to reckon ourselves to be dead indeed unto sin but alive unto God through Christ, (Romans 6:11). Only then can we effectively resist Satan in the name of the Lord Jesus Christ and have him flee from us (James 4:7b).

Sometimes in the early stages, dealing directly with Satan will cause immediate relief in the life of the believer. And, upon submitting to God and reckoning ourselves dead to sin, sometimes there is immediate symptomatic relief, but this is not always the case. Many times God lets us stay down for a while because He has lessons to teach us as we learn to walk in the Spirit. There are lessons for us to learn while we are flat on the bottom as surely as when we are rejoicing on the mountain top. To maintain a faith attitude of victory while experiencing none of the fruits is to begin to learn the walk of faith.

There is the instance of one lady who was told upon

entering into identification with Christ in the first interview that she could expect a satanic onslaught possibly within a week. The next night she called. She had been going through a titanic struggle, and as she described it, the counselor helped her to see that this was a definite satanic attack. She replied that she didn't think it could be because, "It hasn't been a week yet." Sometimes the attack comes hard on the heels of victory.

This regression to self in control varies with every individual just as entrance into identification with Christ varies. Some persons are so diligent in their study of the Word, Christian fellowship, and reckoning upon their position in Christ that they will not tolerate the return of self to control for any period of time. Others are very careless and since there is such relief from the symptoms which they had, they more or less sit back and enjoy it for awhile and coast downhill. They take the attitude almost unconsciously, "Now I can handle myself, Lord." In a short time, they are on the bottom again. There is no need for Satan to intervene directly when the individual is permitting the power of sin to operate in his life.

The author has seen instances in individuals who had experienced identification with Christ without the benefit of counseling and had victory for a period of six months to a year. However, they really didn't understand the dynamics of what God did in their life and how they could claim and appropriate their resources in Christ on a continuous basis. Therefore, they went back under the control of self which remained in the ascendancy for a period of years.

When this is the case, or even if it has been for a shorter period of time, the answer is always the same. Do not try to understand the psychological phenomenon; rather, examine and learn from the circumstances which occasioned the return to self's influence. Whether it is the first, second or twentieth time, the answer for the counselee is to consider himself dead to deeds of the flesh so that Christ might be in control. (Romans 8:13, Galatians 5:24).

Because of ignorance of Satan's methods the author was under satanic attack on occasion for a period of two years after entering into identification. A spiritual pastor prayed and rebuked Satan; the satanic assault ended.

Each successive attack by Satan becomes increasingly more subtle. He wants the individual to think that it is his own failure, not a satanic attack, that is causing trouble. If he can get the process of self-condemnation started again, then it is the downward spiral all over. Satan is as a roaring lion (I Peter 5:8) waiting to devour us if we give him the chance by permitting the flesh again to be in control.

There is no real pattern to the regression or reversion to self. Some of those who have had the worst so-called "mental illness" have had the least regression. Sometimes those who have had the least severe symptoms have had the most by way of regression. Those who have had severe problems know that they can't possibly stand to return to their former way of life. This is probably why they are usually more diligent in their study and fellowship with others and with the Lord Jesus in prayer. Thus, self is continuously dealt with by the cross. This should always be the case with everyone. The counselor must emphasize to the counselee how important fellowship and study of the Word is to the continuing life in identification with Christ. One can't stand idle; he either goes backward or forward.

Each person who experiences Christ in a deep way should be able to share this with other Christians. As he does, he realizes that he must study to be able to express it to others. God permits us to experience "down" times so that we can better understand what others with whom we will be sharing must endure. Otherwise, it might be erroneously inferred that when they have some initial glorious experience, they will be victorious forever after. We should not be experience-oriented. When the Lord Jesus controls the life, there is no need for emotional kicks for the flesh. Christ is our life, and He can live within us on a consistent basis as long as we continually reckon (choose to believe) the self life to be crucified and His Spirit to be in control — another way of saying "Likewise, reckon ye also yourselves to be dead indeed unto sin, but alive unto God through Jesus Christ our Lord." (Romans 6:11)

It is entirely possible for a person's behavior, once self has returned to the ascendancy, to be more defeated than before co-crucifixion became an appropriated reality. It is always good to remind ourselves as counselors and those with whom we share that self never changes from the time we are born until the time we die. Self or flesh is at enmity with God. It can not be changed; it can not be improved. The only proper place for it is death at the cross. Just as Freud and some of his successors have pointed out, all of the experiences of the past remain with us. So long as the self-life has the place of dominance, the habitual manner of behavior will remain a part of our lives. Self and its control are to be regarded as enemies of the believer's victory and are to be treated as a foe that must be rendered inoperative. We must always be vigilant to detect former modes of thought or behavior patterns occasioned by the reign of sin in our lives and to reckon ourselves dead to the power of sin.

In other words, we must keep the "will switch" set on the position which provides power from the Holy Spirit to control our lives.

## SUMMARY

When Christ is in control of the life the believer can expect always to have victory. Second Corinthians 2:14 assures, "Now thanks be unto God which always causeth us to triumph in Christ and maketh manifest the savour of His knowledge by us in every place." This is our birthright through being born of the Spirit. God tells us that we will always triumph in Christ. We need not again live a defeated and frustrated life. When Christ is in control we're victorious. When self or flesh returns to control, we're defeated.

*Satan can only oppress us while we are controlled by self. He cannot defeat the life of Christ in us.* Christ is victorious over Satan and when we depend on our position in Christ and draw upon our resources in Him, we need not fear the onslaughts of the enemy. At the very worst, Satan can only do that which God permits. But if we again take the controls, we can expect to have many of our old symptoms flood back upon us. In fact, it can be even worse when Satan adds some of his own tricks in addition to amplifying old symptoms. We are Satan's prime targets because he fears the witness of Christ to others in our transformed lives. As we share the abundant life in Christ with others, God is glorified. Therefore, Satan tries to shut us down to keep us from bearing fruit and living in victory.

The devil is a defeated foe, and there is no reason for permitting his intrusion into our lives which causes spiritual defeat. The Christian's authority over Satan is clearly stated in Scripture: "Resist the devil, and he will flee from you" (James 4:7b).

Our armor to protect us from the wiles of the enemy is described in Ephesians 6:14-17. Ephesians 6:10 states that we are to be strong *in* the Lord and in the power of His might; verse 11 tells us to put on the armor and verse 13 cautions us to take unto ourselves the whole armor of God that we might be able to stand against the enemy. Pray on the armor; stand in the strength of the Lord; and resist the devil in the name of the Lord Jesus Christ. Then, thank God for His victory.

# Therapy: Bane or Blessing

CHAPTER

10

All of the schools of thought in modern psychology contain some truth, or there would not continue to be clientele which support the therapists in practice. Most of us know persons who have undergone therapy for varying lengths of time who have obviously improved in psychological adjustment. From a human standpoint they have been greatly helped; but the root cause, the self life, has remained untouched. Since the church at large has not shown, and seemingly hasn't known, how the believer may be freed from menacing emotional and mental disturbances, it has turned him over to the medical profession and thereby given rise to

## THE MYTH OF THE MEDICAL MODEL

As one gives serious consideration to the origin of mental and emotional symptoms, it becomes abundantly clear that the preponderance of such difficulties do not originate in malfunctioning glands and organs. The symptoms are in the personality or soul and are a result of a defective spiritual life except in the minority of cases where there is organicity. Over past years it has become commonly accepted that a person with illness should go to a physician. This rationale would make it seem very logical that just as a person goes to a physician for problems in the body he should also see a physician for problems of the mind. And, since the majority of physical ailments have their origin in mental and emotional disturbances, what would be more natural than to have the same man or profession working with both aspects of the problem?

Since the medical profession has been dealing with psychological and behavioral problems for many years, it follows that the general approach to treating psychological disorders would be similar to that used in the treatment of physiological problems. In the realm of the physical, the first order of business is to determine the origin of the problem and to make a diagnosis. After the diagnosis is completed it is possible to prescribe a treatment procedure. If it is determined that the origin of the symptoms is psychogenic (has its origin in psychological conflict) in nature, the person is often referred to another person in the medical profession who proceeds according to type to make a diagnosis of the psychological symptoms and prescribe treatment based upon some recognized classification of mental and/or emotional disturbance. This frequently includes the use of drugs (chemotherapy) in addition to the conventional forms of psychotherapy. Electroshock therapy (EST) is still in use though to a lesser degree than in past years, even though it is fairly certain that some brain damage always results.

Although many thinking persons may question the accuracy of the diagnosis and the type of treatment or therapy elected, very few challenge the necessity of having a medical man deal with symptoms in the soul — the mind, emotions and will.

From the standpoint of the foregoing material, the

psychiatrist who does not perform the role of a spiritual counselor is dealing with symptoms — not root causes. Some would deal with the symptoms purely through the use of psychotherapy, but most would employ some chemotherapy (drugs such as tranquilizers).

It is safe to say that there are very few psychiatrists who use no tranquilizers or other medication for mood support. Conversely, many psychiatrists resort to wholesale use of drugs to assuage symptoms. In one manner of speaking this is a much more honest approach to the practice of psychiatry, since it is obvious to all that this merely keeps the symptoms in check rather than purporting to resolve the problem. Other forms of psychiatry such as psychoanalysis have won acceptance in many quarters on the premise that they get to the "root of the problem." Ministers, likewise, have fallen prey to this ideology and have accepted the inherent dichotomy in treating the soul apart from the spirit. In so doing, they have defaulted on their calling to provide the answer as to how a person may find true peace of mind and deliverance from psychogenic symptoms.

Since psychological conflict is an effect, not a cause, the diagnosis of the spiritual malady or pathology by a spiritual man is of prime importance. It would be mere coincidence if a psychologist or psychiatrist were spiritually equipped to make such a diagnosis; and if he were, he would be performing a spiritual ministry as he allowed the Holy Spirit to do the therapy.

Even though the answer to man's deepest need is not to be found by utilization of the medical model, it is still helpful for a person to understand the antecedent conditions which affect present behavior.

These conditions may be muddied by a mixture of physiological symptoms and it is here that medical training is of utmost importance. Unless these are factored out it is impossible to know just how much is to be treated as psychological overlay. Such things as epilepsy, minimal brain damage, and endocrine dysfunction can prevent the spiritual counselor from giving proper spiritual help. Also, a person in severe psychosis may be medicated to the point where he can be dealt with in spiritual counseling. This type of cooperation between the spiritual counselor and the medical profession is absolutely essential!

Many of those who see the problem as being psychological as opposed to physiological in nature and who elect to work with mentally and emotionally disturbed persons, enter the field of psychology. Even so, the preponderance of psychologists resort to the medical model and diagnose and prescribe a method of treatment or therapy.

Though the fields of psychology and psychiatry differ on many particulars, they generally agree that the origin of the problem is in the mind and emotions as affected by antecedent conditions. However, there is some research to support the thesis that chemical imbalance may cause or contribute to a small percentage of cases of schizophrenia. Orthomolecular psychiatry has emerged as a field of study to deal with such cases and there has been some success with megavitamin therapy.

While conceding that there may be physiological origins to some mental disturbances, it is a foregone conclusion that these would be in the minority. Those who would attribute the origin of mental and emotional disturbances to the domain of the physiological or the psychological fall short of the mark. All of the different approaches to "depth analysis" deal with the mind and emotions but fail to get to the cause — the maladjustment to God and the work of His Spirit, who not only can analyze but also heal and transform the personality. Though analysis purports to reach the recesses of the mind, the writer has seen the Spirit of God recall to a person's conscious mind details of events which years of therapy had failed to surface.

The functions of the spirit of man and its relationship to the soul and body does not fall under the study of medicine or psychology. Rather, only the Spirit of God knows what is in man, so a person who would be used in the lives of disturbed persons must be attuned to the Spirit of God (I Corinthians 2:11,12). This is not to say that there is a premium on ignorance. There is absolutely no reason why a spiritual man cannot master the discipline of psychology and profit by what has been learned and documented concerning human behavior. The fact that psychology offers absolutely *no solutions* to life and its complexities does not prevent its offering some help insofar as the *understanding* of psychodynamics is concerned. The error is in the establishment of psychology as a soul discipline which can purportedly meet man's needs, rather than the use of these behavioral truths to buttress the teaching of the Word of God in the realm of the soul.

It is the position of the author that differential diagnosis should and must give way to the discernment of the Spirit, and that approaches to therapy devised by men must give way to the therapy done by the Holy Spirit through man's spirit which effects a resolution of psychological conflicts in his soul.

## PSYCHOTHERAPY VS. SPIRITUOTHERAPY

The Word of God is very clear in teaching that all of man's needs are to be met in the Person of the Lord Jesus Christ (Philippians 4:19).

It is clearly stated in Philippians 4:6 that we are not to have anxiety, and in verse 7 we are to have peace which is beyond our understanding. The Word of God needs no assistance from a human therapist. To refute this statement would be to charge God with falling short of providing in the Word all that is needed for a sound mind. Furthermore, since psychology as a discipline has developed only in the past one hundred years, it would appear that all of those with psychological disturbances (since the origin of man) were shortchanged by God — if psychotherapy were truly necessary for experiencing a purposeful, satisfying life.

It is obvious that the first-century Christians knew that Jesus Christ alone could satisfy the deepest need of the human heart. In the centuries since then there have been individuals and groups who have understood what it meant to know Christ as their very life. Witness such outstanding Christians as St. Augustine, St. Francis of Assissi, Thomas a Kempis, Madame Guyon, Fenelon, Bishop Moule, et al. The established church in the Dark Ages lost the dynamic of the Christ-life, and the stage was set for the Reformation and the return of the doctrine of justification by faith. During this time there were those who understood and taught the spiritual growth truths, but this never became the major thrust of the movement.

Since the organized church was not known for having the power and resources to meet the needs of men questing for fulfillment and a victorious life, the way was prepared for the philosophers who studied man instead of God. The following chart (Diagram 21) lists a few of the philosophers and the psychological theorists who followed their lead.

Kant, Hegel and Kierkegaard had a major impact in the field of philosophy and their work, among others, created the climate which was conducive to further development of atheistic theories of man's origin, government and destiny as represented in the work of Darwin and Marx.

Similarly, the foundation was laid for the development of atheistic theories concerning the nature of man, his motivation and behavior, and the definition of personality constructs. The most important person here was Sigmund Freud who developed the psychoanalytic theory. Freud has long been known as the grandfather of modern psychiatry, and psychoanalysis is referred to as the First Force in some

## SECULAR THERAPY

Philosophers — Study of Man

1. Kant          (1724-1804)
2. Hegel         (1770-1831)
3. Kierkegaard   (1800's)
4. Darwin        (Physical/Scientific)
5. Marx          (Social/Political)

## PSYCHOLOGICAL THEORISTS

**FIRST FORCE**

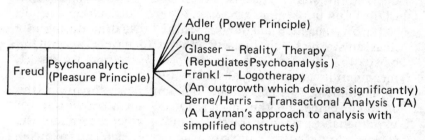

| Freud | Psychoanalytic (Pleasure Principle) |
|-------|-------------------------------------|

Adler (Power Principle)
Jung
Glasser — Reality Therapy
(Repudiates Psychoanalysis)
Frankl — Logotherapy
(An outgrowth which deviates significantly)
Berne/Harris — Transactional Analysis (TA)
(A Layman's approach to analysis with simplified constructs)

**SECOND FORCE**

| Watson, Skinner | Behavior Modification |
|-----------------|-----------------------|

**THIRD FORCE**

| Rogers, | Humanistic Existentialism |
|---------|---------------------------|

**FOURTH  FORCE**

| Cayce, | Parapsychology |
|--------|----------------|

*DIAGRAM 21*

211

psychological circles today.

As the chart indicates, there are many offshoots from psychoanalytic theory. Some are deviations from it; others are in antithesis to it. Whereas Freud's approach emphasizes the pleasure principle, Adler's theory is based on the power principle. Karen Horney would be in the camp of the psychoanalysts but has some areas of conflict with Freud. Jung was a disciple of Freud who later broke with him. William Glasser repudiates the presuppositions of psychoanalytic theory and is diametrically opposed to much of it. Viktor Frankl was a psychiatrist before enduring the deprivation and torturous experiences of the Nazi death camps. His book, *Man's Search for Meaning,* though it falls short of giving the answer in Jesus Christ, does hold that a man must transcend himself if he is to have a meaningful existence. Glasser's book, *Reality Therapy,* likewise is meaningful reading especially when the truths of the cross are superimposed. In this author's opinion transactional analysis as represented in the book, *I'm O.K.; You're O.K.* is psychoanalytic theory translated into laymen's terminology. Whereas Freud utilizes the constructs of id, ego and superego, transactional analysis speaks in terms of your child, your adult, and your parent, which respectively replace the foregoing.

Freud's constructs are a satanic counterfeit of the biblical definition of man as spirit, soul and body.

As it became increasingly apparent that psychoanalytic theory left something to be desired, Watson, among others, began to look at man's behavior and to devise methodology to modify behavior irrespective of the person's early life and psychosexual development. As such, behavior modification became the Second Force in psychology and the banner is still being carried by B.F. Skinner, though his emphasis has changed somewhat in recent years.

As in psychoanalysis, it soon became evident that this

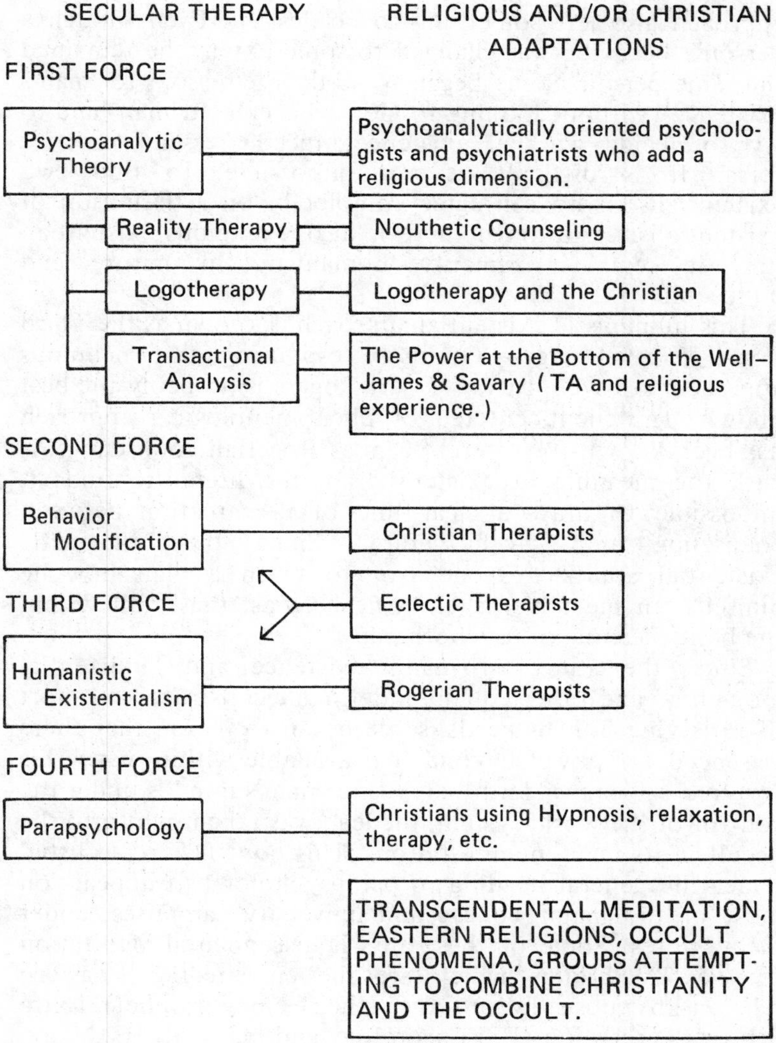

| SECULAR THERAPY | RELIGIOUS AND/OR CHRISTIAN ADAPTATIONS |
|---|---|

**FIRST FORCE**

| Psychoanalytic Theory | Psychoanalytically oriented psychologists and psychiatrists who add a religious dimension. |
|---|---|
| Reality Therapy | Nouthetic Counseling |
| Logotherapy | Logotherapy and the Christian |
| Transactional Analysis | The Power at the Bottom of the Well—James & Savary ( TA and religious experience.) |

**SECOND FORCE**

| Behavior Modification | Christian Therapists |
|---|---|

**THIRD FORCE**

Eclectic Therapists

| Humanistic Existentialism | Rogerian Therapists |
|---|---|

**FOURTH FORCE**

| Parapsychology | Christians using Hypnosis, relaxation, therapy, etc. |
|---|---|

TRANSCENDENTAL MEDITATION, EASTERN RELIGIONS, OCCULT PHENOMENA, GROUPS ATTEMPTING TO COMBINE CHRISTIANITY AND THE OCCULT.

*DIAGRAM 22*

213

approach also left something to be desired. Even though a person's behavior was changed to some extent, he remained the same person. Some began to study the reasons for man's existence (without looking to God who created man) and to try to decide whether existence precedes essence or vice versa. It is difficult, if not impossible, to find two existentialists who can agree completely on a definition of existentialism. Although there is also a religious existentialism, it remains primarily humanistic in nature and philosophy.

This humanistic existential approach is known as the Third Force in psychology. Of those espousing this nebulous approach to psychotherapy, Carl Rogers is probably the best known. His client-centered or phenomenological approach has been known for several years as Rogerian counseling. As with the meaning of existentialism, the literature finds it impossible to draw a clear line of demarcation between counseling and psychotherapy. Since the humanistic existential approaches endeavor to teach a man how he himself can meet his psychological needs, these fall within the basic meaning of psychotherapy.

Since the study of man's existence and "existential moments" and other equally indefinable constructs fell short of satisfying human needs, some began to reason that there was need for power beyond that available within man. This required a "leap of faith" and, since man's mind is under the control of the world system, the leap was taken right into the occult in its many manifestations. This *Fourth Force* is listed under the general heading of parapsychology. It appears on most of the major college and university campuses, under many guises. Some of these are: Transcendental Meditation or the TM groups which are the current rage, Eastern religions, hypnosis, Edgar Cayce (the sleeping prophet), Extra Sensory Perception (ESP), astrology and many others. Many, if not most, of these attempt to look into hidden things and draw upon a source beyond human resources. Since the Word of God is not used as the sole authority and the Lord Jesus Christ is not glorified to the exclusion of all else, this whole area of the *Fourth Force* is related by the author in some dimensions to occult phenomenon.

The following diagram (22) enlarges on the first by adding religious adaptations of several of the forms of psychotherapy. The pattern to date has been for Christians to study various approaches to psychotherapy and adapt these by the use of Scripture, more or less, and calling it "Christian psychology."

Not many years ago the fundamental or evangelical Christian minister was suspicious of psychology and refrained from referring persons for psychotherapy. Now, the evangelical world has turned 180° and has, to all intents and purposes, fully embraced the psychologist who is a Christian without realizing that in doing so the Christian message is often compromised.

A well-known evangelical theologian has publicly asserted that psychologists and psychiatrists have done more to hurt the cause of evangelical Christianity than all of the liberal theologians. However, most Bible schools and seminaries instruct their students to refer those with severe emotional and mental disturbances to Christian psychologists and psychiatrists. While there are Christians who are psychotherapists, there is no such thing as Christian psychotherapy; the two terms are antithetical. The Word of God concludes that self is to be weakened to the point of willingness to accept the fact of co-crucifixion, while strengthening self is the goal of psychotherapy.

The diagram shows that there are men who are evangelical Christians who continue to ply the trade of psychoanalysis which they learned in their psychiatric training. Others may not be trained analysts but are psychologists who give credence to the Freudian constructs of id, ego and superego and operational terms such as the Oedipus complex, castration complex, etc.

Other therapists who are Christians borrow from their secular training and adapt such theories as Logotherapy, developed by Frankl. One such approach has been developed by Dr. Donald Tweedie in his book *Logotherapy and the Christian.*

Another approach to Christian counseling is Nouthetic Counseling developed by Dr. Jay Adams and documented in his book *Competent to Counsel.* In this valuable book he repudiates all forms of psychotherapy and uses Scripture to buttress his positions and in his counseling, and yet he seems to rely heavily upon the approach of Dr. Glasser in *Reality Therapy.* The book is highly recommended collateral reading for those who would do Christian counseling.

As each new approach to therapy is developed, it isn't long until it is adapted or adopted for use in religious circles. Transactional Analysis is no exception. The book which combines TA and Scripture is *The Power at the Bottom of the Well* (TA and religious experience) by James and Savary. Even though Freudian in its presuppositions, many ministers have been deluded by the "simplicity" and employ it to the detriment of their ministry.

The Second Force, behavior modification, also has its adherents in Christian circles. Even though the heart of the gospel message is that behavior change is the result of inner transformation by the Holy Spirit, therapists work from the *outside in* by attempting to modify behavior and change the person. Contracts, goals and other forms of outer-directed motivation are substituted for the inner direction of the Holy Spirit.

Many Christians doing therapy fall into the general Rogerian camp or the Third Force. This approach is less structured and, therefore, less easily identifiable. It supposedly gives more dignity to the individual by assuming that he is innately good or at least capable of finding the answer to his own problem within himself. Of course, these very assumptions are diametrically opposed to the gospel message. The typical Christian who is Rogerian in his counseling approach denies some of the basic Rogerian presuppositions while continuing to hold to the counseling approach or techniques of reflection, etc.

Probably most Christians doing therapy are more eclectic in their counseling. They would borrow a little from the various schools of thought, but the therapy still has the effect of strengthening the self-life.

The Fourth Force, parapsychology, with its many manifestations, finds fewer adherents in the Christian community. Yet there are those who borrow freely from this school of thought. Some are known to use hypnosis while others are majoring in its first cousin, relaxation therapy.

In summary, the therapy scene today involving Christians is an admixture of secular therapy learned from the world system along with varying degrees of scriptural principles to effect behavior change with the net result of strengthening self. The next diagram (23) is a summary and comparison of the world system or the "carnal" weapons with weapons which are "mighty through God to the pulling down of strong holds" (II Corinthians 10:4).

The carnal weapons, philosophy and psychological theories which eventuate in psychotherapy, represent man's best attempt to meet his own needs. The mighty weapons, the Word of God and theology which eventuate in the Spirit's therapy or Spirituotherapy, represent God's all-sufficient and only method of meeting man's total needs in the person and work of the Lord Jesus Christ.

It is tragic that usually a mentally or emotionally disturbed person who is unable to care for himself and who has no one to take responsibility for him must submit to some form of psychotherapy in an institutional setting. May God hasten the day that such persons will be able to elect spiritual counseling in a similar setting.

II Corinthians 10:4
(For the weapons of our warfare are not *carnal,* but *mighty* through God to the pulling down of strong holds;)

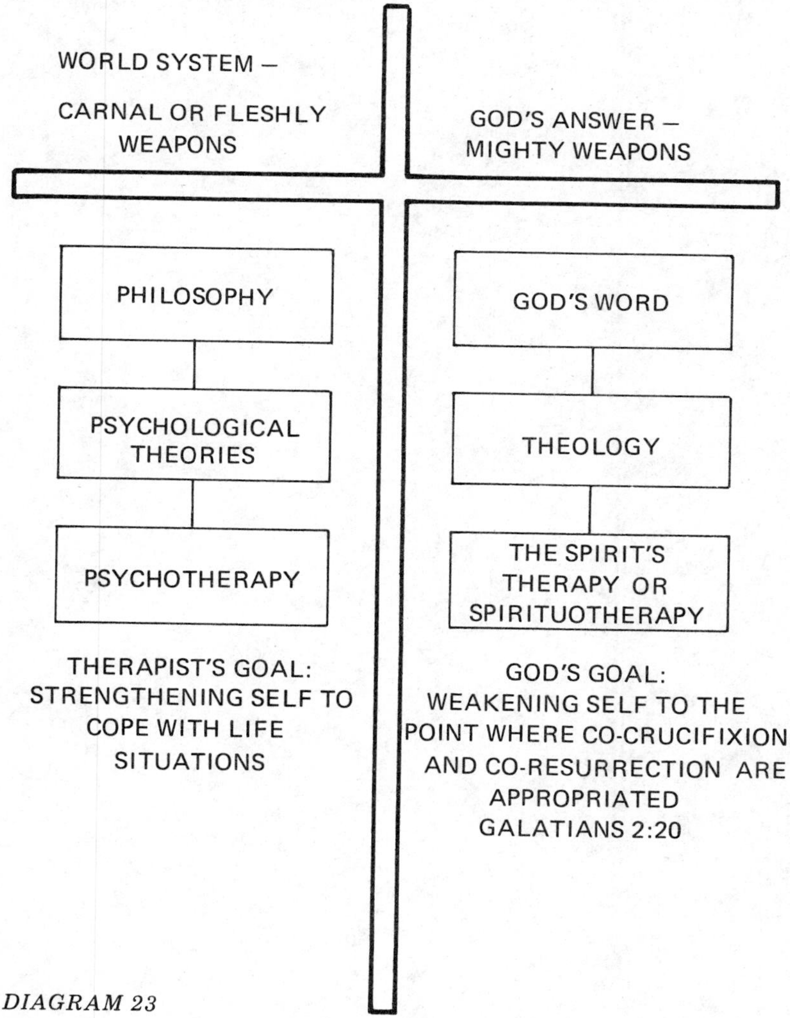

WORLD SYSTEM —

CARNAL OR FLESHLY WEAPONS

GOD'S ANSWER — MIGHTY WEAPONS

PHILOSOPHY

GOD'S WORD

PSYCHOLOGICAL THEORIES

THEOLOGY

PSYCHOTHERAPY

THE SPIRIT'S THERAPY OR SPIRITUOTHERAPY

THERAPIST'S GOAL: STRENGTHENING SELF TO COPE WITH LIFE SITUATIONS

GOD'S GOAL: WEAKENING SELF TO THE POINT WHERE CO-CRUCIFIXION AND CO-RESURRECTION ARE APPROPRIATED GALATIANS 2:20

*DIAGRAM 23*

# An Open Challenge to "God's Tattered Army"

Second Timothy 2:3,4 states, "Thou therefore endure hardness, as a good soldier of Jesus Christ. No man that warreth entangleth himself with the affairs of this life; that he may please him who hath chosen him to be a soldier."

The obvious comparison here is that those who are in the service of our Lord have much in common with the members of a military organization. Each has a commander-in-chief who is charged with the responsibility of over-all strategy, timing, selection and training of personnel, goals, discipline, etc.

It is imperative that the commander-in-chief understand the enemy, his strengths and weaknesses, and his method of operation. Under-estimating and over-estimating the resources of the enemy are equally disastrous.

Before a military operation is begun it is necessary to chart the objectives of the campaign and to count the cost in terms of personnel, materiel and time which will be expended to reach those objectives. After everything is considered, there must be the belief on the part of those initiating the operation that there is a better than even chance of victory, assuming there is responsible leadership.

Until recent times there has been unquestioning obedience of military personnel to their superiors such that the organization may function with a unity of purpose making for effective use of all resources. When there is not the absolute necessity of pulling together for purposes of survival, there is frequently grumbling and internal dissension which drastically reduces the effectiveness of the organization to carry out assignments. Also, when the objectives are indistinct and ill-defined, and there is no commitment on the part of the country to push for total victory, there may be wholesale desertion and/or avoidance of becoming part of the army at all.

We have seen the foregoing carried out in real life in the military operations in Indo-China. Individual rights, a near absence of morality, loss of confidence in government, drugs — these and other symptoms combine to all but stifle any semblance of a disciplined military machine.

The breakdown in the moral fibre of our military is common knowledge, but it is actually representative of the decline in morality in our country and, for that matter, the world. The gravity of the situation is underscored in the United States, since we have borne much of the responsibility for evangelizing the world due to having the resources and freedom to proclaim the gospel of Jesus Christ.

All of the indicators — economy, ecology, government, military, ideology, morality — combine to prove that we have very little time left with the freedoms we have known unless some drastic changes are made soon. These changes can not be carried out by the secular community since the basis for the changes must be transformed lives on the part of those involved.

Only God is in the business of transforming lives so this

means that the church is the organization and organism whereby the changes must originate. But what is the likelihood that the church can be mobilized to perform the task? What is the situation that obtains within the church as it undergoes inspection by our Commander-in-Chief?

If we look at all the facets of Christianity in the country, we find that the record of the various units pulling together to accomplish *anything* in the past has been all but non-existent. The writer knows of no joint effort on the part of *all* denominations, churches and church groups which has been successful. Those programs which have been successful which were across denominational lines have been largely in the area of social concern, both in this country and abroad.

This article is not for the purpose of endorsing an ecumenical position relative to church government or polity. It is, rather, to point up the urgency of reaching our country and the world for Christ on a scale which will have a profound effect on government in this and other countries. Such an undertaking will require that God's "army" consist of disciplined, obedient, healthy, mature Christians who are more devoted to carrying out the orders of the Commander-in-Chief than to in-fighting and riding hobby horses.

We can not sacrifice our obedience to the Word of God and still be virile Christians, but we can not refuse to work together toward the common goal of reaching the world for Christ and be within the will of God.

Many have become so secular on the one hand or so parochial on the other that they have lost sight of God's vision for the world. The victory has already been won and we have but to enter into that victory by faith and, in obedience, carry out the mission with which we are charged.

But what of our soldiers — are they trained, disciplined and ready for battle? Do they know the enemy, and are they prepared to engage him? What has been their success in the small skirmishes? Have they passed the test on home ground in basic training, or were they washed out as 4F before boot camp?

From the casualties seen in the counseling office, it is apparent that the rank and file Christian is all but unable to stand in time of peace and not at all prepared to withstand the rigors of battle. The conflict is not for children but for mature Christians. Likewise, the spiritually diseased and infirm are a liability rather than an asset in the heat of the battle.

The immature and/or neurotic Christian may wave the flag and be highly desirous of being obedient to the Lord but is ill-equipped to do so. Before the church is going to have a significant impact on this country and the world, there must be revival among Christians. Those who are weak and sickly must be faced with the message that the Word of God speaks to mental and emotional symptoms as well as to defeat and discouragement. The hour is late and the options are rapidly narrowing. Those who have gone to the world system for the answers and have depended upon the world system for the "good life" are soon to find that their source of supply is drying up.

As the enemy mounts his offensive the Christian and consequently, the Church can capitulate or, ". . . having done all, to stand" (Ephesians 6:13). The best defense is a good offense, but the army must be combat ready and properly outfitted. As of now, exactly the opposite is true. Too many are immature, unhealthy, flabby, disorganized, and fighting amongst themselves with very little, if any, recognition of the life and death struggle in which the church is engaged. In the lives of most Christians it is "business as usual" without sufficient spiritual sensitivity to perceive the conflict and without the total abandonment to Christ which is the *sine qua non* of the victorious life.

Sir Malcolm Muggeridge of England who recently became a

Christian has been involved in the news media most of his life. With sufficient knowledge and wisdom to appraise the world situation, he likens the citizens of the Western World to a group of frogs in a pan which is being heated over a fire in a container of water. The frogs are lulled into an attitude of lethargy and complacency as they become warm and drowsy. By the time the water begins to boil, jumping from the pan would do little to remedy the situation.

It is increasingly apparent, even to those outside the Church, that it will require a spiritual awakening if our country is to survive as a free nation. Only as we mature and abound spiritually are we going to be able to provide the world leadership which can stave off chaos and despair.

If we are Christians, we have been born into "God's Army". The question then is, "Will we submit to His sovereign leadership and let Him equip us by filling or controlling us by His Spirit to carry out the task ahead?" Just as the Lord Jesus Christ was born to die, we must lose our life if we are to find it (Luke 9:23,24). Resurrection life follows crucifixion; if we are to know the "power of His resurrection," we must first be made "conformable to His death" (Philippians 3:10). At our new birth we partook of His life (John 5:24) and of His death (Galatians 2:20; Romans 6:6) that we might be "seated with him in heavenly places" (Ephesians 2:6).

Only those who have appropriated their death with Christ are really prepared to live. Those who have not are "carnally minded" and are "dead" while they live, since "to be carnally minded is death" (Romans 8:6). Death is separation from the source of life. If we are not abiding (John 15:5) in Christ who is our life (Colossians 3:4) which produces a renewed (Romans 12:2), or spiritual mind (Romans 8:6), we are living as though dead.

Walking in the Spirit (Galatians 5:16) is God's intended norm for the Christian life; the alternative is to walk "after the flesh" (Romans 8:13) which can only produce the works of the flesh (Galatians 5:19-21). Conversely, walking in the Spirit produces the "fruit of the Spirit" (Galatians 5:22,23).

Our Lord's parting promise was that we would receive power "after the Holy Spirit had come upon us" and that we would be "witnesses" unto Him (Acts 1:8). The world is seeing so little of the power of the Holy Spirit that most Christians are witnesses unto death rather than unto life. In a world that is crying out for love and life, the unsaved are seeing Christians fighting among themselves rather than encountering the common enemy. Instead of saying, "See how they love one another," they have every right to say, "See how they hate one another." Before we can offer a solution to the world, we must demonstrate that we have been delivered from the power of sin — not just in our words but in our living. We must love others — beginning with "the household of faith" (Galatians 6:10) if we are to earn a hearing for the gospel before the unsaved.

Even though we are going out under the banner of the cross lustily singing, "Onward Christian Soldiers," we will not be marching on to victory unless we are abiding and resting in Him who is Victor.

We have our marching orders; the trumpet has been sounded. The equipment has been issued, the training made available, and all power is given unto Him who said, "I am with you alway, even unto the end of the world" (Matthew 28:18-20).

While the battle is raging and men are dying without Christ, many Christians go about their daily tasks oblivious to the battle and to their responsibility. The enemy continues to press his advantage until "the water begins to boil."

The hour is late. The need is now. With the world at its worst, we must be at *His* best!